Advance Praise for
A Summer Like That

"At once romantic, thought-provoking, and poignant, *A Summer Like That* explores what happens when a mother's fierce determination to protect her child coincides with her equally fierce desire to protect her heart. Lo's vivid descriptions are a feast for the senses; I found myself craving roast goose with plum sauce, crispy oyster pancakes, and mango pudding long after I turned the final page. Straddling class differences and cultures, Leo and Pearl's love story had me cheering for them every step of the way, and Win-Win's sweet, thoughtful nature drew me in from the start. Everyone should have A Summer Like That — one where a fairytale comes true, and the life you always longed for is finally, at long last, within your grasp." — Emily Colin, New York Times bestselling author of *The Memory Thief*

"Jane Lo examines the undercurrents of place, politics, and family demands in *A Summer like That*. She sensitively and insightfully dissects the often-unspoken tension between a Hong Kong man and a mainland Chinese woman who struggle to find simple acceptance, love and harmony. Will the opposing forces of family and societal expectations be insurmountable?" — Kelly Kaur, author of *Letters to Singapore*

A SUMMER LIKE THAT

"In *A Summer Like That*, Jane Lo weaves a tale of heartbreak, unexpected connections, and the healing power of new beginnings. Set against the backdrop of sweltering summer days in Hong Kong and the bustling tourist city of Xiamen, the story follows Pearl, a local kindergarten assistant, and Leo, a heartbroken teacher from Hong Kong. Their lives intersect when Leo, seeking solace from a devastating breakup, meets Pearl, who is striving to make ends meet by posing as a tour guide. As Pearl introduces Leo to the vibrant life and hidden corners of Xiamen, an unlikely friendship blossoms. Pearl, with her optimism and resilience, slowly helps Leo find a way to mend his shattered heart. Through their shared adventures, from ferry rides to Gulangyu Island to the breathtaking sunsets from Sunlight Rock, they discover that sometimes, healing comes from the most unexpected places. Lo's writing is rich with vivid descriptions and emotional depth, capturing the essence of both the locale and the inner lives of her characters. Her narrative style, blending humor with poignant moments, makes this novel a compelling read. *A Summer Like That* is worth reading for its beautifully crafted characters, evocative setting, and heartfelt message about the power of human connection and the possibility of new beginnings." —Jane Houng, author of *Under Lion Rock, Asian Elephant Art, Cat Soup and Other Short Stories*

"*A Summer Like That* is a wonderful love story, driven by the reality of a complicated world, and filled with moments of real charm. Leo and Pearl are such wonderful, compelling characters. Spending time with them is so rewarding." —Caitlin Jans, author of *Incident Reports*

JANE LO

"Jane Lo skillfully immerses readers into family relationships evoking a blend of sadness and humour. Her portrayal of the difficulties of a cross-border relationship beautifully highlights cultural and lifestyle differences." — Anjali Mittal, author of *The Boat Race*

"Jane Lo's compassion and generosity of spirit are reflected in her stories. Her themes are universal: love, family, discovering oneself, making and unmaking decisions. That's why her stories mean something to all of us. Who hasn't been in similar situations? In this book, Leo has to make a decision that will direct the course of the rest of his life. We follow him anxiously, wanting only the best for him, believing that we know what that best is. But then, Lo twists the conclusion, making his decision more real and relevant than the reader could ever have imagined." — Constance Lieber, author of *Dr. Martha Hughes Cannon: Suffragist, Senator, Plural Wife*

"*A Summer Like That* has all the key ingredients of an engaging love story, but it is Lo's keen eye for the cultural conflicts and social prejudices between Hong Kong and mainland Chinese that adds timely social commentary along with spice to this charming romance." — Heather Diamond, author of *Rabbit in the Moon*

"In *A Summer Like That*, Jane Lo masterfully weaves together the lives of two strangers, crafting a poignant tale of connection and healing against the backdrop of cultural contrasts. Lo's vivid descriptions and authentic characters draw readers deep into a world where the warmth of human kindness shines through personal struggles, delivering a touching exploration of love, loss, and unexpected friendships." — Jiksun Cheung, author of *The Precipice and other stories*

A SUMMER LIKE THAT

"Jane Lo is a master of getting to the heart of the human condition. In *A Summer Like That*, she has another winner of a story that will stay with you season after season." —Susan Blumberg-Kason, author of *Good Chinese Wife and Bernardine's Shanghai Salon*

"*A Summer Like That* weaves a disarming narrative about losing and finding love, as well as the leaps of faith and courage necessary to form an enduring partnership. As the main characters—Leo and Pearl—struggle with pressures from family and friends, the novel also thoughtfully examines the complications of language, culture, and class across the seeming divide of Mainland China and Hong Kong. Jane Lo offers a delightful and intelligent reimagining of the romance genre, one that engagingly melds explorations of the heart with insightful social commentary." — Dr. Tara Lee, instructor of writing and literature at the University of British Columbia

"Jane Lo's *A Summer Like That* is a heart-warming story of two people who find love when least expecting it—a story of hope and second chances just when we're ready to give up. I found myself wanting a 'Pearl and Leo' sequel!" —Rinkoo Ramchadani, author of *A Fistful of Feet and other stories*

A SUMMER LIKE THAT

JANE LO

A Summer Like That

By Jane Lo

ISBN-13: 978-988-8843-95-4

© 2025 Jane Lo

FICTION

EB223

Cover art by Eugenia Volobueva

All rights reserved. No part of this book may be reproduced in material form, by any means, whether graphic, electronic, mechanical or other, including photocopying or information storage, in whole or in part. May not be used to prepare other publications without written permission from the publisher except in the case of brief quotations embodied in critical articles or reviews. For information contact info@earnshawbooks.com

Published in Hong Kong by Earnshaw Books Ltd.

Prologue

If I had to break a teacher's heart, I would do it in early November, when term marking is at its peak, compositions piled sky-high. Or perhaps in late January, after mid-year examinations, when teachers everywhere are drowning in that great sea of unmarked scripts, when life's purpose is reduced to meeting the mark entry deadline.

Because it is bad enough to have the love of your life break things off with you over instant noodles and red bean milkshakes at Café de Coral, to have her reject your offer of a lifetime together before you even had a chance to ask, to have her shatter your heart into so many pieces you know with crushing certainty that it will never again beat the way it did.

It's bad enough, isn't it, without it happening to a teacher at the start of a suffocating Hong Kong summer, with sweltering days that bleed into sleepless nights which spill back over into bleary-eyed days, an endless uninterrupted cycle in which your broken heart has your undivided attention for weeks and months on end.

I would not wish a summer like that on anyone.

Chapter 1
Pearl

There didn't used to be so many tourists in Xiamen, but now they were everywhere—mostly tourists from other parts of China, but also foreigners. They explored the city with their noses buried in their maps and travel guides, selfie sticks at the ready. Having never left Xiamen, I felt that having the tourists bring the world to me was a good thing. When I was waiting for clients at the ferry terminal, I liked to listen in on their conversations and try to guess where they were from. I was in the minority, though. Most locals tolerated the tourists as a necessary nuisance.

The ferries to Gulangyu Island were a particular point of contention. Locals and tourists alike used to be allowed to purchase tickets from Lundu Terminal and ride the same ferries, but eventually the numbers of tourists grew unmanageable. The municipal government proceeded to build the tourists their own 'international' terminal, considerably further out, about a twenty minutes' walk from Lundu. Most of the tourists were unaware of the change, though, so they continued coming to the old terminal, only to be turned away. In the sweltering heat, twenty minutes was a very long walk.

A SUMMER LIKE THAT

This was where I—and a great many other otherwise unemployed locals—came in, eagerly waiting to offer our services. For a small fee, I brought the tourists with me to the ticket counter at Lundu Terminal as my friends or relatives, purchased tickets on their behalf, and took the short ferry ride with them to Gulangyu. On the way, if I could speak their language, I usually offered a little introduction to the UNESCO heritage site. If they wanted, I could even serve as their tour guide for the day, although these days most tourists liked to explore on their own. I then made my way across the strait back to the terminal, where I waited for another tourist to be refused a ticket.

It was not a particularly glamorous or exciting way to spend a summer morning, or an entire summer's worth of mornings, but I told myself I was playing a small yet significant part in Xiamen's growing tourism industry- though my role was not, of course, officially sanctioned and if I were caught I'd have to pay a hefty fine. I hadn't been caught yet.

I was on a ten-month contract at the kindergarten and drew no income in the summers. Ba sent Ma care packages from Shanghai once or twice a year, but that was about it. I saved up as much as I could during the school year for me, Ma, and Win-win, but our budget was still pretty tight in the summer months. Earning what I could as a friend of the tourists helped.

Win-win was not a demanding child; he was happy enough eating Ma's cauliflower and sliced pork stir-fry every day and wearing hand-me-downs. Still, it'd be nice to be able to bring him to McDonald's every now and then, and I often wished I could buy him some nice things. I'd seen the way he eyed that red scooter at RT-Mart, the one with the Spiderman design across the handlebars. He taught himself how to ride on the neighbor's bike; he wasn't even five yet.

Ma normally took care of Win-win when I was working,

but the whole neighborhood was going to Third Aunt's home tonight for her first grandchild's full-moon celebration, and Ma had promised to help with the cooking once I got home. This was no problem; there weren't many tourists so late in the day.

I was just about to head home when he approached me.

The first thing I noticed about him was his facial hair: he was sporting a patchy beard which made it difficult for me to guess his age. If I had to guess, I'd say he was somewhere in his forties. I didn't know anyone in real life who wasn't clean-shaven, and this man's beard wasn't neatly trimmed, like the ones I'd seen on television. His looked sort of wild and unloved, as though it had come about unintentionally and then been forgotten. He was wearing a blue T-shirt with a faded picture of a soup can on the front, and khaki shorts that had cargo pockets on the sides. The overall effect was one of neglect.

'Can you please tell me where I can catch a ferry to Gulangyu?' His clumsy, accented Putonghua gave him away immediately: he was from Hong Kong. His eyes were bloodshot, as though he was suffering from some kind of allergy or hadn't been sleeping well. Or maybe he'd been crying, who could say?

'They won't sell me a ticket.' He tapped his watch, one of those bulky fitness trackers, and frowned at what he saw. 'I really need to get to Sunlight Rock in time for the sunset. Is there any way I can make it?'

'I can take you there.' I was very pleased. Ma would forgive me for being an hour late, surely. 'Tourists can't purchase tickets from this terminal, but I'm from here. I can help.'

He cocked his head, surprised. 'That's very kind of you,' he said, clearly flustered. 'I really shouldn't take up your time. If you could just show me where *I* can buy -'

'Please, I'd be happy to help.' I lowered my voice a little then, leaned in a tiny bit as though I was about to reveal a secret.

A SUMMER LIKE THAT

Experience had taught me that this was the best way to pitch my service. 'I normally charge 100RMB for a round trip on the ferry, but since it's already so late, would—'

He nodded in understanding. I wasn't offering my time out of kindness; this was a business transaction. It was alright to accept. He nodded, taking out his wallet and handing me 100RMB. 'Thank you.'

The ticket seller didn't seem to notice, or care, that this was to be my seventh trip across the strait that day. Her eyes were on her cell phone as she handed me 30RMB in change and the two round-trip tickets. She was watching an old episode of *Meet Your Match*, my favorite matchmaking programme. I knew how that episode was going to end: that beautiful Chongqing girl, Qinqin, will finally meet her match after months on the show with no luck.

There weren't very many passengers on the ferry with us; we had our pick of seats. The man opted to sit near the front, where the wind was the strongest. I didn't mind. The customer was always right.

'My name is Pearl.' The engines were so loud I was almost shouting. 'And if you want, you can speak Cantonese. I can understand.' I smiled. 'I love to watch TV. The Hong Kong soaps are the best!'

When he responded, it was in Cantonese: 'I'm Leo.'

'Like the actor in Titanic!' I was delighted. I loved that movie so much, especially the part when Jack and Rose are at the prow of the ship, their arms outstretched. It was so very romantic. 'Is it your first time in Xiamen? How do you like it?'

'Yes, first time.' He smiled a little at me, politely, then continued looking out on the water, at Xiamen's skyline. Under ordinary circumstances, this was when I'd give him my little introduction to Gulangyu, but he clearly had no interest, which was fine with me. I surreptitiously typed a message to Ma and Win-win so they wouldn't be worried. Ma responded almost immediately with a photo of Win-win blowing me a kiss. In the background was Third Aunt's dining table, a dish of red birthday eggs arranged into a pyramid. I breathed a sigh of relief; that was alright, then. When I looked up again, I saw that Leo was still staring at the waves.

By the time we arrived at Neicuoao Terminal, it was nearly 5:30. I gave him a moment to take in the beauty of the island — its vermillion roofs; its beaches, the sand so fine it was like cake flour, along the shoreline; the way the narrow paths twisted this way and that — before glancing meaningfully at my watch. 'We're going to have to hurry to catch that sunset,' I said. He nodded.

I led the way up a steep stone path towards Sunlight Rock. There was an easier route, but it would take us an extra ten minutes, which we didn't have. He bought two tickets at the foot of the Rock, and we ascended the three flights to the small viewing platform, perhaps five meters in diameter, at the top. A sizeable tour group armed with phones and selfie sticks were already gathered there, but we managed to secure a spot along the far end of the railing. He dropped his backpack at his feet and took out his phone from his back pocket. I watched as he fiddled with the settings and took a few shots.

The sky was no longer blue, but that glorious pre-sundown purple, streaked with pinks and oranges. Thankfully, though, the sun was still a good distance from the horizon. I could tell from experience that it was gearing up for its descent; we probably only had about fifteen minutes before nightfall, maybe less. Ma always said the sun looked like a salty egg yolk at this time of day. The thought made me hungry for Xiaobei's full-moon feast. Below us, the waves crashed lazily, halfheartedly, against the Rock.

A SUMMER LIKE THAT

'We made it,' I said, lightly.

He turned to me, nodding. 'We did indeed. Thank you. You were very quick.'

Again, there was that sense that he was finished with the conversation. We watched silently as the sun dipped lower and lower into the water below, the tour group around us commenting noisily on its beauty. He took shot after shot. I could tell he was not a professional photographer; the pictures kept turning out blurry. His hands were shaking too much. I thought of asking if he was cold, perhaps even offering up the windbreaker I had in my backpack. But that seemed absurd; the back of his T-shirt clung to him, dark with sweat.

Night fell abruptly and the streetlamps on the island all came on at once. The tour group behind us let out a cheer when their guide announced that their next stop was the renowned seafood restaurant on Gulangyu, Xin Yu. 'Watch your step, please!' the tour guide cried. 'This way, everyone!'

My stomach rumbled as I imagined a seafood feast at Gulangyu's finest restaurant. I laughed nervously, hoping Leo hadn't heard. I didn't want him to feel guilty about the time.

'I guess it's over,' I said, smiling at the man.

This was met with silence. I was about to say something else, something about how it was getting late, that I needed to head home, but he kept staring out at the water, even though there was nothing to see anymore. He didn't apologize as he wept soundlessly beside me, the emotion so tightly constrained that just watching him made my heart ache.

I felt my phone buzz in my pocket: Ma, or maybe Win-win, calling from Ma's phone. 'Excuse me,' I said quietly. I backed up a few meters towards the top of the stairs. There was no longer anyone one else on the viewing deck.

It was Ma. In the background I could hear a baby wailing.

'Where are you? It's past seven! Why aren't you here yet?'

'Sorry I'm late, Ma.' I glanced at the man, saw in the darkness that he was still hunched over the railing. 'I'm alright, it's just the client, he's—'

I heard her sharp intake of breath. 'Are you in trouble? Shall I send one of your cousins?'

'No, no trouble. I'll be back in about an hour. Please tell Third Aunt I'm sorry.'

'Okay. Win-win wants to talk to you.'

A pause, then, my son's sweet, lilting voice: 'Mama?'

'Hi, baby. Sorry I'm late.'

'It's okay. I ate two red eggs already. I saved you one. I peeled it for you and put it in my pocket.'

I stifled a laugh. 'Thank you. How's Xiaobei?'

'Not too good. He just keeps crying. Ah Meh wants her phone back now. Bye, Mama.' I could hear the sound of the phone being passed from one hand to another.

'Pearl? I have to go. Huilan's *babao* rice pudding didn't turn out right and she's frantic, thinking of making taro mud instead.' Ma sighed. 'I don't think she has enough time, told her she should just serve fruit at the end of the meal, but she won't listen. Anyway. Be careful. It's getting late.'

I considered leaving the man where he was and just heading back. He wasn't my responsibility. I brought him here like I promised, didn't I? And the ferry tickets were return tickets. He could find his own way back to the mainland.

But then I thought of the way his shoulders shook as he wept, the way he kept taking blurry photographs because he couldn't hold his camera steady. I'd never seen a man cry like that before.

Anger was the only emotion Hong showed when he learned I was pregnant with his child. He abruptly announced that things were over between us; he didn't want that kind of burden on his shoulders. I told everyone it didn't matter—we would have broken up anyway, the bastard just beat me to it—but it had hurt to be discarded like that. It wasn't till Win-win arrived, months later, that my heart stopped aching at the thought of Hong and the future—really, just the security—we might have shared. My son was nearly five now. Somehow, we had made it this far.

But Leo was alone in a foreign city, obviously upset about something—was it love, like it was for me?—and I felt an emotion I couldn't quite name churning within me. Pity? Worry? I didn't know.

I walked back towards the railing and rested my head in my hands for a moment, as though I was enjoying the view. Finally, I took a deep breath. 'Leo?'

He cleared his throat, turning away from me. 'It's time to go, isn't it? You go ahead. I'd like to stay here a little longer.'

'Sure,' I said, as though that was alright with me. 'I'll be going then.'

'Okay.' He didn't move.

'But... but do you have plans for dinner?' My own forthrightness surprised me, but I plunged ahead. I leaned in a little, the way I always did for a pitch, although this was unlike any pitch I had ever made. 'I was wondering...it's your first time in Xiamen, right? Wouldn't you like to experience a traditional Xiamen meal? Families in my village always celebrate a baby's first full moon with a feast, and as luck would have it, my aunt—'

He smiled a little, the way he did. 'You're very kind, but no thank you. I'm sorry to have taken up so much of your time. You should hurry back for your aunt's feast. Thank you again.'

'No,' I said, desperately. 'You misunderstand me. There's no charge for this. I'm inviting you to dinner at my aunt's house. She's quite a good cook,' I continued, grasping at straws. 'Her grandson, Xiaobei, is very cute, and he's one month old today.

Don't you want to meet him? Please come.'

'Thank you, but—'

I took one final stab. 'It's so dark. I... I don't feel safe going home so late by myself.' This was a lie; I had headed home from Gulangyu much later than this. But beneath his sorrow, I could sense in Leo a kindness, and I knew before I asked that he would not be able to refuse. The words continued tumbling out of me: 'Will you take me home?'

At this, he finally scooped up his bag.

Chapter 2
Leo

I felt as though I was in some kind of travel documentary as I took the ferry, then a crowded bus, then another even more crowded bus, with this woman I had just met. We were going to her village for her baby cousin's full-moon feast.

I could see the programme's title in my mind's eye: Hong Konger in Xiamen — The *Real* Experience. I did not volunteer to be cast in this role, though, and I wished I could be heading back to the hotel instead. I didn't understand why Pearl had insisted on inviting me to her aunt's home. For a few moments on the ferry, I wondered whether she might be some kind of con artist, but she didn't have that look about her. On the contrary — I'd never met someone so earnest, so sincere. I considered myself a pretty good judge of character, and I didn't think she was trying to scam me.

If this really were a documentary, I would be chatting with her, asking questions about her way of life and her views on her city. I would ask her for recommendations on the best restaurants, the best local street food stalls. As it was, she didn't need any prompting from me; she had been talking and talking. Every few minutes she checked her phone for messages, sometimes pausing to take a selfie and sometimes taking a picture of the view outside the bus window. 'For my mother and my son,' she explained cheerfully, even though I hadn't asked.

My plan had been to travel through China by high-speed rail this summer, and this was only my third stop after Shenzhen and Guangzhou, but I already thought I might be ready to go home. The plan to lose myself in the mainland wasn't working; I missed Lindsay as much as ever, maybe even more than before. I couldn't seem to stop taking those stupid sunset photos for her although I had enough sense to know not to send them to her.

We used to collect them; Lindsay used to say we needed lots of sunsets so we could have an entire wall of them in our bedroom one day. She really said that.

Some nights, when I'd been lying awake in bed for seven, eight hours in an unfamiliar Chinese city, I would wonder if I'd made it all up. The sunsets, the weight of her interlocked fingers on the back of my neck, the way she used to say 'I love you, I love you, I love you,' just like that, three times, instead of goodbye, when it was time to hang up. The one advantage of being in mainland China was my inability to go on Facebook and see what she was up to, but that was about it. My brother Henry was good at IT stuff and would have been able to help me get a VPN, but of course I hadn't told him where I was headed this summer.

'Leo,' Pearl was saying, 'have you tried *shaoxiancao* yet? Some people say it's best with sweet potato balls and red beans, but I like it plain, just with syrup. Nothing to interrupt the silky texture of the jelly! You know, there is a very good place for *shaoxiancao* right by our house. I'll point it out to you when we get off the bus. Another local dish you really must try is the oyster omelette, which is the yummiest thing in the world. I wonder if Third Aunt cooked that tonight, I really hope she did, I think you might like it, but if she didn't, I'm sure my mother would be happy to fry some up for you—'

Pearl loved to talk. She spoke to me in Putonghua, and I responded, when I had to, in Cantonese, each of us speaking in the dialect that we were more fluent in. I wasn't sure if she talked so much because she saw herself as some kind of ambassador for her city, or if she pitied me. I knew she had seen me crying on the viewing deck after the sunset. I'd been wondering what Lindsay had done with those pictures we took together, all five years' worth of them. Were photographs recyclable? Or had she just thrown them in the garbage?

Pearl didn't ask any questions about where I was from, or what I did, or what I was doing in Xiamen. It was almost as if she knew I couldn't talk about it. I'd never met anyone as enthusiastic about her hometown as this woman, but that was fine by me. The last thing I wanted to think about was home.

Her village was small, just seven or eight homes in total, all constructed of stone and neatly arranged into two rows with a walkway, perhaps two meters wide, between them. The village was dark but for one brightly lit two-storey house at the end of the road. 'That's my aunt's home,' Pearl said eagerly. 'Everyone's there for the celebration.'

She broke into a little run, but quickly turned around again to make sure I was following her. 'Come on,' she said, beckoning. 'You must be hungry. I know I am!'

'Mama, Mama,' a little boy's voice cried as we approached the house. It was an outdoor party: there were maybe thirty people in all, gathered around four round tables set up in the courtyard. The tables were covered in red plastic tablecloths and crowded with orange plates heaped high with food. I saw a dish that looked like it might be the promised oyster omelette. Having had no appetite in days, I was surprised to find that Pearl was right: I was hungry.

In Hong Kong, a baby celebration could be a very extravagant affair, a twelve-course banquet with ten or fifteen tables' worth of guests. That was certainly the case for Corrie, my niece, when she turned 100 days old. My fussy sister-in-law had insisted on holding the banquet at the Peninsula Hotel. It was absurdly luxurious for such a little baby. They had given everyone Swarovski rabbits as party favors, an over-the-top nod to Corrie's Chinese zodiac sign. Henry told me afterwards that they had not even spent that much on their wedding.

Everyone was speaking animatedly in the local dialect, which I did not understand, and there seemed to be children everywhere. Some people peered at me curiously, but without ill will; no one seemed to mind that I had walked in on their party. Pearl waved at two women—one had to be her mother, Pearl looked so much like her—who were bringing out more food from the house on metal trays.

A little boy suddenly barreled into Pearl. She hugged him close. 'This is Win-win,' she said, finally releasing him. She spoke in Putonghua, rather than their dialect, for my benefit. Her eyes were bright with pride. 'Win-win, this is Uncle Leo.'

Immediately he turned to me, bowing his head. 'Leo *Shushu*,' he said softly. He had greeted me the way his mother asked, using the generic term for uncle, *Shushu*, that catch-all for all unrelated adult male figures in a child's life. He held onto his mother's hand.

'Hello, Win-win,' I said, crouching in front of the little boy. Win-win looked as though he'd walked out of a children's storybook: his face was perfectly round, his cheeks bright pink, and he was sporting the quintessential bowl cut. His eyes were like the inverted 'u' eyes of a smiley face emoji, and he looked very much like his mom. A memory surfaced of Lindsay saying she wanted all boys, no girls.

'Very nice to meet you. How old are you?'

He immediately held up four fingers on one hand and a thumbs up with the other. He was tall for his age, about the same height as Corrie, who had just turned six. I wondered where his father was.

'Four and a half,' I nodded, understanding. He was tall for his age then. A few children had gathered around us, a dusty soccer ball at their feet. I surprised myself when I motioned to Win-win to throw it at me. When he did, I juggled it on my head like a seal — five, six, no, seven! times — before allowing it to slide gracefully onto my right shoulder, down my arm, and onto my right hand. I proceeded to spin the ball on my index finger, to the great delight of the children, who by this time were clapping and cheering. When I felt the ball slowing down, I tossed it gently to Win-win, who caught it with both hands against his chest. He smiled shyly at me. Hearing their applause, I felt a small spark of life within me — something I hadn't felt in a very long time.

Pearl led me to one of the tables and handed me chopsticks and a bowl. 'Eat more, eat more,' everyone told me in Putonghua, although they didn't know who I was. They gestured enthusiastically at the food on the table. Upon closer inspection, I saw that most were half-finished already; we had arrived very late for the meal.

'Win-win is very cute,' I said quietly to Pearl.

'Thank you.' She smiled. 'You are good with the little ones.'

Pearl introduced the dishes to me as she spooned a little of each into my bowl — an egg that had been dyed red, the promised oyster pancake, braised duck, pan-fried fish, a cauliflower and pork dish, two kinds of fried sausage, one fish and the other chicken—and someone poured me a glass of warm beer. I ate everything, drank everything. The food was cold but good. No one asked what I was doing there, and I didn't explain. I wasn't sure I understood what I was doing there, either, but for reasons I couldn't quite articulate, even to myself, that seemed okay.

Pearl milled about, chatting. Someone began blasting Mandopop music on their phone. The children danced. The women served guava wedges and hot tea; the tea was better than anything I had ever had in Hong Kong. Some of the men started playing a noisy drinking game, and though I was invited to join them, I declined, opting to watch instead.

Later, one of the men—presumably the baby's father—disappeared inside the house before reemerging with a mysterious box, which turned out to be filled with a special surprise: firecrackers and fireworks. I was surprised by how adept even the little ones were at handling the sparklers, at the little candy-sized fire crackers Pearl called little goldfish, which had to be thrown on the ground to release their spark and pop. In Hong Kong fireworks and firecrackers were forbidden by law, so I had never played with them before. I watched nervously as the children and adults alike flitted about, throwing handfuls of little goldfish on the ground to make little explosions, or drawing shapes in the air with their sparklers.

'Don't be afraid,' Pearl laughed, noticing my trepidation. She handed one glowing sparkler to me. 'It won't hurt you.'

After we had burned through the box, everyone got a turn at holding the baby, even me. The young mother smiled shyly at me as she placed Xiaobei in my arms. He was warm and heavy, a big baby. I had always thought by the time I turned 40, I would be a father already.

'Xiaobei is so cute, right?' Pearl was beside me again. The party was ending. Everyone was helping out with the tidying up, even the children—it was a noisy, cheerful affair of clearing away bowls and plates, stacking stools and putting away folding tables. Win-win and another little boy dragged brooms across the courtyard in an attempt to sweep up the peanut shells and firecracker packaging.

'Pearl, thank you.' I felt my voice catching in my throat. I swallowed hard.

She shrugged a little, smiling. 'Welcome to Xiamen.'

Chapter 3
Pearl

'Mama,' Win-win said, yawning, 'can I sleep in your bed tonight?'

He asked me this every night after his bath. I used to say no, thinking I shouldn't coddle him too much. A little boy with no Baba needs to learn more quickly than ever to be strong and manly, doesn't he? But I finally decided it wasn't worth the two hours it took to calm him down and dry his tears only to have him climb out of his crib in the middle of the night and sleep on the floor beside me.

It was pretty late already, past ten. I stayed behind at Third Aunt's to help with the last of the cleanup, and Win-win insisted on waiting up for me.

I zipped up his sleeping bag, the yellow one with the rabbit on the front and holes for his feet. I loved this sleeping bag; it made him look like a baby.

I kissed him on the nose. 'But once you turn five—'

'I know, I know. When I'm five I'll be a big boy, and big boys *always* sleep in their own beds, right? I know that, Mama.' He nodded earnestly. 'But I'm still four now.' He held up his four fingers. No thumb.

A SUMMER LIKE THAT

When I finally nodded, his face broke into a broad grin. He grabbed his pillow and climbed into my bed. Almost immediately he slid off the bed again and waddled across the room to his crib; he couldn't move very fast in his sleeping bag. 'I forgot Wuwu,' he said guiltily. He hugged his well-worn turtle to his chest as he rushed back to my bed.

It was a bit of a squeeze, our two pillows side by side on my twin bed, but Win-win knew the trick—he always slid half of his thinner toddler pillow under mine so they mostly fit, mine sticking out just a couple of inches. He snuggled under the covers, even though he was wearing his sleeping bag. He pulled the blanket right under his chin, content.

'Good night, baby,' I said, kissing his forehead. I switched off the light and slid on the floor to sit beside him. Win-win rolled over a few times, then stilled. I waited for his breathing to become regular, then slipped back out into the living room.

The television was on, the volume turned low. Ma and I sat on wooden stools in front of it. Between us was a third stool with two orange melamine bowls on it—one nearly overflowing with peanuts, the other empty and ready for the shells. We spent every night together like this.

Meet Your Match was on. When it wasn't, we watched re-runs; we were both obsessed with the programme and knew the previous eighteen seasons practically by heart. It wasn't that I necessarily wanted this kind of happy ending for me—I knew better than to believe that I had to depend on a man for my happiness—but it was fun to watch. A bit like watching a Hollywood film or a soap opera, except this felt a bit closer to reality. Sometimes the production crew would interview matches made on the programme a year or even five years later—and seeing the couples still in love filled me with a sort of hope that maybe some people really are destined to meet their match.

The current bachelor was sloppily dressed in a black undershirt and jeans ripped at both knees. So far only two women had kept their lights on for him to indicate their interest; the other twenty-two switched theirs off right off the bat. I doubted he'd last much longer. He didn't have the right look for the programme; the women tended to favor professional-looking men with stable jobs with good prospects. This guy, a 27-year-old from Changsha, had a rather ugly tattoo of a dragon on his left shoulder which extended to his neck. 'I'm a freelance musician,' he was saying. 'I love rock and roll.'

Sure enough, about thirty seconds into the family and friends video, right after his brother began discussing the bachelor's vast knowledge of imported wines and spirits, the two lights went out, almost at once. The host, my beloved Shiu *Yeye*, graciously thanked the bachelor, who took his walk of shame offstage amid suitably depressing music ('Love is not that easy—') and muted applause.

The next bachelor, neatly dressed in khakis and a navy dress shirt, looked a bit like Leo, mid-forties, with a beard. Ma noticed, too. 'This fellow looks like your friend,' she commented mildly as she cracked open a peanut with her thumbnail.

'Yes,' I murmured, my mouth full. The introductory remarks revealed that this bachelor's credentials were not particularly impressive—32, from Shenzhen, a manager at a handbag factory, and enjoyed open water swimming—but all 24 women kept their lights on. 'He really does. He even has a beard.' This bachelor's beard was a lot neater than Leo's.

'Pearl,' she said, glancing at me. 'Are you interested in him?'

'No way. I just met him at the ferry pier. He's a client, from Hong Kong.'

A SUMMER LIKE THAT

She raised one eyebrow. 'Hong Kong?'

I nod. 'It's his first time here. Maybe he'll hire me for another job.' This was unlikely; he didn't even have my number. Earlier that evening, after everything was cleared away—Leo had insisted on staying till the end to help stack stools and fold up tables, perhaps as a thank you—I walked him back to the bus stop. I worried only a little that he might get lost on his way back to the hotel—he would have to remember where to get off by himself, but he could always ask the driver. I was still contemplating giving him my number when the bus came, and then he was waving goodbye to me from the open window.

What I had felt was not romantic attraction, but relief that he was going to be alright. Ma finally put the peanut in her mouth. 'I just want you to be careful, daughter. You know how you can be.'

I didn't like how she was alluding to Hong, to that disaster of a relationship. I kept my eyes fixed on the television and sort of grunted.

'I know you'll be careful,' she added, patting my hand. 'Look, Pearl, Nana's saying yes.'

Nana Wang, the twenty-six year old CEO from Ningxia, was leaving hand-in-hand with the bearded bachelor. Nana blew a kiss of thanks at Shiu Yeye before leaving the stage for the last time, to thunderous applause. In the background, Andy Lau crooned about the kind of love that lasts ten thousand years.

Chapter 4
Leo

Later that night, when Henry called, his voice sounded different, as though it had travelled a great distance to reach my ear. The first thing he said to me was: 'What are you still doing up there? Come home.'

'I told you I'd be gone all summer.'

'Sure, but it's been three weeks and you haven't called home even once. Mom's really worried.' He cleared his throat. 'So am I.'

'I'm fine.' And it was true—I'd just gotten back to the hotel from that dinner at Pearl's village and I felt almost alive again for the first time in weeks. Deep down I had hoped the fog that had settled around me after losing Lindsay would clear eventually, but I had no idea how long it would take. The whole summer? A year? More? But tonight the fog had lifted, at least a little. In fact, I'd been thinking about Pearl when Henry called. I was thinking that her son's eyes were exactly like hers—they looked like the eyes of a smiley face.

'Lindsay called.'

My legs wobbled beneath my weight. I sank onto the foot of

the double bed. 'Oh?'

'She called Mel earlier today, asking if you were doing okay.'

Dating my sister-in-law's high school BFF had been a bad idea from the start, but knee-deep in love, I hadn't cared, and I certainly hadn't thought through the implications if we were ever to break up. I thought we were in for the long haul, and it wasn't just me — Lindsay and Melissa had often giggled about becoming sisters one day too. Now, there was nothing funny about it; I felt exposed and ashamed. What had Lindsay said to Melissa about me? No one in my family knew that I had proposed, only that we had broken up.

'Oh.' The fog threatened to descend once more, and I fell on my tried-and-true method for righting the world whenever it began to spin on its side: I recited the alphabet backwards in my head. *Z. Y. X. W.V...*

It kept on spinning, so I frantically changed tack — I tried to remember things Pearl had said to me: *Gulangyu is home to 193 historical buildings.* Shaoxiancao *is best enjoyed plain. Ma makes great oyster pancakes. You are good with the little ones. Hold this — it won't hurt you.*

'Anyway,' Henry continued hastily, interrupting the silence, 'where are you now?'

'Xiamen.'

'That's nice.' Henry clearly had no idea where this was; he had never been anywhere on the mainland. Neither had I, until last month. Our parents had always opted for family trips elsewhere — like many Hong Kong people, Thailand, Taiwan, and Japan were their favorite destinations. I could remember many childhood summers spent at some beach resort in Phuket or Pattaya. Although Shenzhen was right across the border and easily accessible by MTR, they had never taken us there. I had never really given much thought about it until now.

'Yeah. It's pretty nice here.' I hesitated. 'Thanks for calling. I'll send Mom and Dad a message in a minute.'

'Great.' He cleared his throat. 'When do you plan on coming back?'

I have no idea, I was tempted to say. 'Henry, don't worry. I'm fine.'

I hung up and sent Mom a picture of the giraffes at the Guangzhou Zoological Garden. I didn't know what to say to her, so I kept my message brief: *HI MOM!!!* At the last moment I threw in a heart emoji. She would like that.

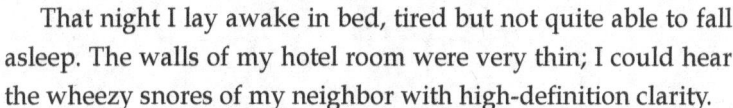

That night I lay awake in bed, tired but not quite able to fall asleep. The walls of my hotel room were very thin; I could hear the wheezy snores of my neighbor with high-definition clarity.

As was my usual practice at that hour since the breakup, I prodded at my broken heart with memories of Lindsay: her nails, always manicured, always a pale peach; the smell of her hair (peony); the little mole on her right eyelid. My eyes still smarted when I remembered the way she used to kiss the top of my head, how she used to reach it by kneeling on my thighs. There was no denying that my heart was still sore, but I was surprised to find the worst of the wound seemed to have scabbed over. When had that happened? *How* had that happened?

My hands shook as I unlocked my iPhone. I studied the sunsets I'd collected in the past two weeks with a critical eye: in Shenzhen, atop Ping An Finance Centre, the fourth tallest building in the world, and in Guangzhou, from the window of a cable car on Baiyun Mountain. The sunset I saw with Pearl at Sunlight Rock was the most beautiful of the three, but the photos were blurry. I thought about the way Pearl stood beside me, quiet, as I took the pictures. I thought about the way she invited me, so tactfully, to her relative's home for dinner, as though she knew I needed help.

In a moment of weakness — or was it courage? Who could say? I deleted them all.

Chapter 5
PEARL

The next morning was Saturday, my busy day at the ferry terminal, my day for making up the shortfall from the week. I enjoyed the challenge, relished the opportunity to use my skills and hard work to earn enough for my family. I had a feeling it was going to be a good day.

It was early; Win-win and I woke up together just after 6am, shortly after he wet the bed. He still did that sometimes, but after the first time it happened, I had lined the mattress with a plastic shower curtain, so it wasn't too much trouble to change the sheets.

I fixed Win-win and myself our breakfast—a steamed bun each with a bit of condensed milk, and warm soy milk—and listened as he told me about his dream from the night before. His brows were furrowed.

'...and then, Mama, Wuwu hid in his shell, like this,' here he tucked his head into his chest, 'even his tail, Mama, he even hid his tail, but the fox came closer and closer, and Mama—' He slipped his hand into his mouth, sucking on his third and fourth fingers the way he'd done since he was a baby. I could see his eyes begin to well up, but he swiped at them fiercely. 'But finally the fox went away and then Wuwu was safe. And then I woke up. That was my dream, Mama,' he let out a great sigh, the anxiety over. A moment later, he began gnawing at his bun again. 'Did *you* dream?'

Dreams were a new development for Win-win; he had only started telling me about them in the last month or so. I remember the way he woke up that first time, his eyes bright, and told me that there had been a movie playing in his head while he was sleeping. *It was a good movie, Mama, but not a cartoon.*

I had dreamt, but the dream — an unsettling mess of Hong, Leo, and the bearded bachelor, all keeping their lights on for me in a jumbled-up version of *Meet Your Match* — was not something I wished to revisit with Win-win. 'I can't remember it very well,' I lied. In fact, I could remember every detail, down to the gaudy fuchsia dress I was wearing, its horrible sequined neckline. When I woke to find Win-win had wet the bed, I felt relief rather than annoyance: I wouldn't have to find out how the episode ended.

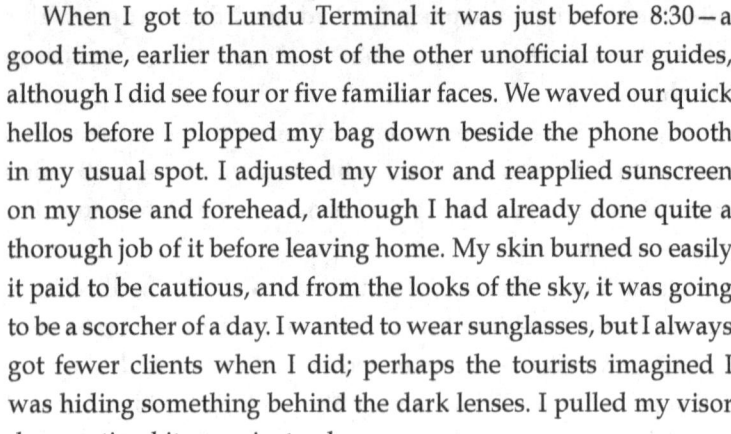

When I got to Lundu Terminal it was just before 8:30 — a good time, earlier than most of the other unofficial tour guides, although I did see four or five familiar faces. We waved our quick hellos before I plopped my bag down beside the phone booth in my usual spot. I adjusted my visor and reapplied sunscreen on my nose and forehead, although I had already done quite a thorough job of it before leaving home. My skin burned so easily it paid to be cautious, and from the looks of the sky, it was going to be a scorcher of a day. I wanted to wear sunglasses, but I always got fewer clients when I did; perhaps the tourists imagined I was hiding something behind the dark lenses. I pulled my visor down a tiny bit more instead.

JANE LO

At first I didn't recognize him—cleanshaven, he looked much younger, and his gait was different, too, he wasn't dragging his feet the way he had the day before—but he kept walking closer and closer, and finally, when he was about twenty meters from the phone booth, I saw that it *was* Leo, waving at me. I waved back, eagerly. He looked great, almost a different person. Even his clothes were brighter—today he was wearing a lime green T-shirt with a few English words across the front.

'Hi,' he said, his expression bashful. 'I was wondering if you could tell me where I can get a ticket for Gulangyu?' He laughed. 'I'm just kidding. Morning, Pearl.'

'Good morning,' I said, pleased. 'What are you doing here?'

'Actually, I was hoping I'd bump into you,' he said, a little apologetically. 'I'd like to do some sightseeing, and you mentioned yesterday that you sometimes take tourists to the sights. I wondered if you'd be willing to do that for me. At cost, of course.'

This took me by surprise. 'You seem different today,' I said, hesitantly. 'You seem... happier.'

'I am,' he said, his expression earnest. He was silent for a moment. 'For weeks I felt like I was stuck. Like I would always be stuck.' He paused here, staring at the cracked tiles beneath our feet. 'I don't feel as stuck today,' he said quietly, finally lifting his gaze to meet mine. 'Thank you.'

I was moved by this. I couldn't remember the last time I heard a man speak in this way. Had I ever? Hong was always putting on macho man airs. In my ignorance, I had mistaken that for self-confidence. How wrong I was.

Had Leo not been a stranger, I would have patted his hands comfortingly and assured him that everything was going to be okay. That's what Ma would have done. But I had only just met him the day before. Instead, I smiled. 'You're so very welcome. I would love to show you around Xiamen. There's so much to see! There's the old fortress at Hulishan, of course, and the seafood market, and Xiamen University is said to be the most beautiful university in all of China. And it really *is* very beautiful, definitely worth seeing. The *tulou* are a bit further from the city centre, but everyone who sees them says they're worth the trip, and Xiamen Botanical Garden has got so many cactuses, it looks like an actual desert in there, and —'

'Pearl,' he interrupted me, gently, 'I trust you. You lead the way.'

He smiled then, and it was a real smile, one that reached his eyes. Unexpectedly, I felt my heart constrict.

Silly, I told myself. *Stop being silly.*

Chapter 6
LEO

Even though Pearl had one of those two-headed portable fans wrapped around her neck—the kind Lindsay and I had mocked endlessly when they came out the summer before—sweat was rolling down the sides of her face. She stopped walking to mop her face with a limp striped towel before fiddling with the controls on the fan's bendy arms so the whirring from the fan heads was louder, the blast stronger. I could feel it from where I was standing, and contemplated, for the first time, buying one of those fans for myself. What Lindsay would say if she saw me!

When I started fanning Pearl I with a map of Xiamen from my bag, her smile was sweet. 'Thank you so much,' she said, lifting the ponytail from the nape of her neck and dabbing at her neckline. 'Don't mind me. I take after my mom; we're both miserable in the heat. This here is Zhongshan Road,' she added, pausing to gesture at a wide shop-lined thoroughfare. 'Normally it would be our first stop, it's in all the guidebooks, but most of the shops and restaurants won't be open till after noon, so there isn't much to see yet.'

She led me instead onto a bus with *Xiamen Botanical Garden* flashing in LED along the front and sides. 'The Botanical Garden is probably my favorite place in Xiamen,' she said, sitting down near the back of the bus and patting the seat beside her. I sat down. The bus was only half full today; everybody apart from us was poking at their phones. 'It's beautiful there. There's one area that's nothing but cactuses. You'll love it. Lots of locals buy the annual pass and visit on the weekends. It's so much nicer than the zoo. Although Win-win doesn't think so.' She rolled her eyes, grinning.

'I'm excited,' I said, and I was pretty sure Pearl could tell I meant it, because she smiled at me, indulgently, the way she probably smiled at Win-win when he was looking forward to an outing. Without warning, she held up two fingers in a peace sign and snapped a selfie, then quickly sent it with a message on her phone.

She laughed. 'Sorry. During the summer Win-win's always asking where I am, what I'm doing. I can't always call him during the day when I'm working, so I got in the habit of sending my mom these pictures. You know, to let him know I'm thinking of him. Them, I mean.'

I liked the idea. 'Sounds like a great way to stay in touch.'

She nodded. 'Want to take one with me? I'm sure he remembers you and will be excited to see you.'

I leaned in a bit closer and made my trademark silly face: eyes crossed, tongue out. I saw the split-second of surprise in Pearl's eyes before she rearranged her features to match my expression. Pearl smelled faintly of sunscreen, a smell I associated with holidays and happy times.

'Let's take another one,' she said, giggling as she saw the picture her mom and Win-win sent in response. It matched ours perfectly.

This time, Pearl just smiled, scrunching her nose a little. I did the same.

JANE LO

The Xiamen Botanical Garden turned out to be a staggeringly large place—Pearl said it was exactly 4.93 square kilometers. When I recognized this number for what it was—nearly *seventeen* times the size of Hong Kong's Disneyland—I felt almost faint. A vivid memory of Lindsay lip-syncing to 'A Whole New World' as we watched the fireworks in front of the princess castle together tried to surface but I shook my head roughly, clearing my head of it.

Pearl brought me to the different themed areas, introducing the various plants species with surprising detail. 'How do you know all this?' I asked.

She blushed, then quickly recovered, waving a dismissive hand at me. 'It's nothing. I love plants, and anyway, I've read the visitor's guide a hundred times.'

We saw several couples dressed in full wedding attire, their photographers calling out instructions (*'Place your left hand on her lower back! Look longingly into each other's eyes! Do not show so much teeth!'*) as they snapped picture after picture. The most popular spots for the wedding shoots seemed to be the Bamboo Forest and the Rose Garden, but I agreed with Pearl that the dubiously-named 'Psammophytes Area' was the highlight of the park. I had never seen so many cactuses in my life, nor did I expect to be so charmed by them, but it was hard not to with Pearl so eagerly introducing each species, taking special care to show me her favorites.

'Can you take a picture of me for Win-win?' she asked. She handed me her phone before I could respond. She posed with the sea of cactuses behind her, her hands daintily holding up the sides of her white sundress as though she was preparing to curtsy.

I realized then that she was very beautiful.

Chapter 7
Pearl

It was a very warm afternoon. Even beneath my UV-protection umbrella, the top of my head was hot to the touch. I kept reapplying my sunscreen but my nose was beginning to feel sore. It was almost certainly burnt. Leo hasn't complained about the heat at all, although every now and then I saw him fanning himself with the visitor's guide.

I had already given Leo a brief history of the Hulishan Fortress and pointed out the two most interesting cannons — the German-made Krupp, which was an impressive 2.8 meters in length and held the world record for being the oldest and largest cannon of the 19th century, as well as the world's smallest cannon, which was only 11cm long and weighed just half a pound.

He listened to all this politely, and even took a few pictures of the cannons, but I could tell that history was not a particular point of interest for him. Frankly, neither was it for me. I was beginning to wonder whether we should have skipped the fortress and headed straight for Xiamen University, but it would have seemed negligent to not have brought him here at all. Hulishan was an important part of Xiamen's history, and while I may have been a freelance tour guide with no license, I did have standards.

We had been strolling idly for several quiet moments when he broke the silence: 'Have you always worked as a tour guide, Pearl?'

I shook my head. 'Not at all. During the school year I'm a teaching assistant at my son's kindergarten. The teachers are paid year-round, but the assistants and other support staff don't get any salary during the summer.' I shrugged. 'I guess it's only fair; we don't have the same qualifications. In the summers, some of my friends from the kindergarten work in RT Mart, others work as servers in restaurants. As for me,' here I placed a hand over my heart, and paused dramatically before saying, 'as for me, I found my true calling as a tour guide.' I was inordinately pleased when he let out an appreciative laugh. 'It's not terribly stable work, but I like it.'

We reached a few stone benches that were in the shade of a gingko tree. I sat down on one and patted the seat beside me; it was wonderfully cool. When Leo sat down, I noticed that his toenails were trimmed so short they must hurt. Hong was the complete opposite; as a child his mother had heard that it was good luck to have talon-like feet, and since the age of about five he had grown out his toe tails. I found them monstrous. Looking at them used to make me feel queasy.

'I'm a teacher, too,' Leo said. 'I don't get to work with little ones, though. I teach in a secondary school.'

'Oh, I'm not really a teacher.' It was kind of him to assume I am, but it wasn't true. 'I just help take care of the children. You know, bringing them to the washroom and making sure they stay in their cots during naptime when their teachers are on their lunch break, disinfecting their toys at the end of the school day, that sort of thing.' I laughed. 'It sounds dull, but it's actually not bad at all, and the best part is I get to see Win-win all day. Of course I'm not supposed to give him any special attention.'

He smiled. 'Of course not.'

'I always have to remind him not to call me Mama during the school day. He's supposed to call me 'Teacher Chen' like everyone else. I'm always reminding myself not to give him extra hugs and kisses, too. And definitely no extra fruit at tea time.' I looked sheepish. 'Sometimes I wish I could though, especially when it's Friday. They get watermelon every Friday, and that's Win's favorite.'

Leo's eyes crinkled into slits when he laughed. I felt my heart flutter in my chest as he did. He looked so young and worry-free this way. I wanted to keep telling him stories so that he would keep laughing.

'What about you? What do you teach?'

'English,' he said, simply. He shrugged. 'Honestly, I don't know enough about anything else.'

He acted like it was nothing, but I was impressed. 'I tried so hard to learn English when I was younger. I even went to a language centre, can you imagine? It cost me so much money! But everyone said English is the key to finding a high-paying job, so I thought it was worth it. My classmates picked it up so quickly,' here I snapped my fingers, first on my left and then on my right, to show just how quickly, 'but for me the words just wouldn't stick. My teacher said I didn't have the right ear for learning English.' I laughed, remembering the way Miss Alicia would blow her bangs every time I made another blunder. I attempted to mimic her now: '*Pearl, it's three thirty three, not free firty free!*'

The memory made me giggle, especially because my tongue still tripped over the consonant clusters that had given me so much trouble back then. 'Anyway, I've kept up my 'self-study' by watching Hollywood films. I think I'm doing pretty well. *You jump, I jump*, right?'

Leo didn't laugh. 'How can someone not have "*the right ear*" for learning a language?' He put the offending words in quotation marks, and I had to hide my smile. How serious he had suddenly gotten, over nothing. 'That's the most ridiculous thing I ever heard. She should've found another way to help you learn, not laugh at you. How unprofessional to treat you that way. Shameful.'

He sat silently beside me and I could feel the anger emanating from him in waves. What would it be like to be his student? He could be so serious, but kind, too. When I snuck a glance his way, I saw that he was glaring at the bench across from us, as though my teacher from five years ago was here at Hulishan with us. I patted his arm tentatively, the way I did with my mother's arm when someone had upset her, and especially if the offender was still in the room with us. 'It was so long ago, Leo. She didn't mean to be unkind. Never mind. Anyway, I *do* remember a few things. *Long time no see! Wanna grab a coffee?* Not bad, right?'

I saw his lips twitching, as though they were trying hard not to give way to a smile. 'Not bad at all. You speak beautiful English. You make me *wanna grab a coffee*.' He said the last few words in English, with a straight face, but his eyes were twinkling.

I burst out laughing, then pretended to pout. 'Hey, no teasing!'

'Sorry, sorry.' He grinned sheepishly, holding up his hands in surrender.

I poked him in the arm. 'Just kidding. Anyway, the certificate from the course did open some doors for me, so it was worth it. I got that job at the kindergarten. I was new, but they still gave me a few months of maternity leave when Win-win came.'

Leo nodded. 'That's great. In Hong Kong, women only get sixteen weeks. My sister-in-law nearly quit her job after she gave birth to my niece, she was so mad about having to go back to work when Corrie was only 10 weeks old.'

I thought of Win-win as a tiny bundle in my arms and felt a bit weepy just imagining having to go back to work that soon. 'I would've wanted to quit, too.'

'I've been meaning to ask you about Win-win's name. Is it an English name?'

I smiled. 'It is and it isn't. It's a bit of a long story, but when Miss Alicia found out I had given birth to a boy, she suggested I name him *Winston*, after the famous British leader. She was from England, you see. It was perfect because my mom had already decided that his Chinese name was going to be *Bo'wen*, you know, 'to strive for knowledge', and that had the same sound, 'wen'. And I like the meaning of the English word *win*.' I realized this was the first time I had really explained any of this to anybody. 'That's what I want for Win-win. Not to be a loser, but a winner.' In my mind's eye I could see Win-win as a man: someone who could hold his head high, someone who had the world as his oyster. Someone nothing like his father. I was alarmed to find my eyes welling up. I looked away, pretending to study one of the cracked tiles on the ground in the distance. 'I really want my son to win at life.'

For several moments, neither of us spoke. Then, without warning, Leo's hand was on mine. When he spoke again, his voice was earnest: 'He will, Pearl. He will.'

When was the last time a man touched me?

Before I could count the exact number of years, his hand had returned to his lap.

By the time we left Hulishan, it was nearly 3:30. 'We can go to the seafood market now, or maybe visit one of the universities?

JANE LO

There are fifteen universities in Xiamen, isn't that incredible? The best known and most beautiful is Xiamen University, of course, but if you prefer —' My voice trailed off as I saw Leo glancing at his watch.

'Why don't we head back to your village?'

'Now?' This was not what I wanted to hear. I would have only brought him to two spots. I realized then that I hadn't discussed the terms of my services to him, and that I hadn't asked him to pay 50% of the tour guide fee upfront, the way I would normally have. The time we'd been spending together didn't feel like work, and he wasn't like any client I'd ever had, but still, money was tight. I hadn't even given Ma any money for groceries yet, and Win-win's sandals were so small, his toes stuck out the front and were always getting scraped when he was on the neighbor's bike.

He must have noticed that I was frowning, because his voice was gentle, playful even, when he continued: 'You did say there's a dessert place worth checking out by your village.'

'There is, there is,' I said, still flustered, 'but I thought we were on a full-day tour.'

He stopped walking then, and swung his bag around so he was wearing it on his front. He dug around in his bag for a moment before yanking out his wallet, a brown leather one that looked as well-worn as his watch.

'I'm sorry. I was going to pay you first thing this morning,' he said quickly. He pulled out a wad of 100-yuan bills. Was that ten bills? More? It was far too much. 'I meant to, but we got to talking, and I —'

'That's not what I meant,' I protested, struggling not to get upset. It *was* what I meant, but I could feel my cheeks burning with embarrassment. I didn't want him to think that I had only been showing him the sights for his money. Although, hadn't I been? I switched on my fan and kept pressing the button until it was on full blast; its familiar whirring helped me clear my head a little.

'I'm not sure what you normally charge for day tours, but you've been a wonderful guide. Please, accept this.' He kept holding out the bills to me, his head bowed. 'Is 1,000 yuan suitable?'

'We've only been to two spots. I only charge 500 for a full day.' I was shaking my head. This talk of money was making me uncomfortable. I haven't been treating him like I would a client; have I ever taken a selfie with one, or told them the story of Win-win's name? Still, when had I ever refused a client's money? 'I'll accept 250 yuan.'

'Pearl,' he said, his voice earnest. 'Please accept it all. It's what I would have paid an agency, and you've been better than any agency.'

He placed the bills, gently, in my hand. I blinked, realizing that my eyes are welling up once more. I was ashamed, but also grateful. He hadn't said *You could really use it*, which would have been entirely true.

'I've upset you,' he said, his brow furrowed, clearly flustered. He dug around in his backpack again. His hand re-emerged with a packet of tissues. He handed me one, his head bowed. 'I'm sorry.'

The tissue was peach-scented; it smelled like candy. I had never used such a sweet-smelling tissue before. It made me smile. 'Thank you.'

'I'm sorry,' he repeated, penitent. 'Please, may I take you home now?'

———∞———

When we arrived at the mouth of the village, I saw Win-win

riding our neighbor's son's bike in front of our house. The seat was much too high for him, but he was managing. What I really needed to do was to get him a helmet. A helmet, and a new pair of sandals.

'That's Win-win, isn't it?' Leo asked. 'He can ride a bike already? A big one like that?'

False humility was common in our culture, and some mothers might have said *Oh, it's nothing*, but it wasn't nothing to me. Far from it. 'He taught himself,' I said unable to hide the pride in my voice.

Leo let out a low whistle that made me swell with pride.

As we approached our courtyard, Win-win saw us and waved eagerly. He slid off the seat and the bike crashed to the ground behind him. I'd warned him a hundred times about taking better care of things, especially borrowed things, and was about to call out a reprimand when he ran back to it and propped it up, carefully, against the gate before running towards us again.

I scooped Win-win up in my arms; he'd gotten so much heavier in the past year but for now I could still manage. He clung to me, koala-like. He fished out some unshelled peanuts from his pockets and fed them to me.

'Leo Shushu?' Win-win cocked his head, as though unsure whether it was really Leo. When I set him back on the ground, he held out his palm to Leo. 'Want a peanut? Ah Meh grew them.'

Leo took one, tossed it high in the air, then caught it at the last moment in his mouth. 'Tasty!'

Win-win giggled, making me giggle too. Leo bowed theatrically, then plucked another peanut from Win-win's hand and repeated the trick. He could be so silly. For a moment I remembered how forlorn he had been just one day before. I didn't really want to think about that.

Leo held up the bag of takeout we picked up on our way

home, and Win-win's face lit up. Watching my son jump up and down, I couldn't help but feel a surge of warmth for Leo, who was the one to suggest picking up some fries and McNuggets for afternoon tea. He lay everything out on the square stone table in our courtyard, using the paper bag as a makeshift tablecloth. Win-win was practically drooling, but still he waited patiently until Leo had finished squirting out the ketchup packets and said, 'Enjoy.'

Ma emerged from the house, her hair tied up in a handkerchief as usual. 'You're so early today,' she said to me. She glanced at Leo, Win-win, and the little spread of fast food, before continuing with, 'Won't you stay for dinner?' I knew she'd say this; in our village, hospitality as a value was second only to filial piety.

That night, she prepared a hearty meal: meatball soup, *miangua* noodles, stir-fried cauliflower and pork, and a luxurious surprise, no doubt to impress our guest—a gleaming oyster omelette. At first I wondered if these dishes would be considered humble in Leo's eyes, but to both my and Ma's pleasure, he asked for seconds, and seemed to be genuinely impressed by Ma's cooking: 'I've never had noodles this fine' and 'This cauliflower is so tender.' People were normally so stingy with giving affirmation; I could see Ma glowing beneath his praise.

Leo's comment about the cauliflower was especially pleasing because Ma had harvested it from the field just that afternoon, and an easy conversation about her crops flowed, even though she was normally rather reticent around strangers.

After dinner, she invited Leo out to look at her prized rows of carrots, sweet potatoes, cauliflower, shallots.

'I would love to,' he said, standing up immediately.

I stayed behind to clear the table, but Win-win scurried after them, and slipped his hand into Leo's. My heart constricted again, and this time I didn't force myself to pretend I hadn't felt it.

As I was scraping the remaining food into a single motley dish to be heated up for Ma and Win-win's lunch tomorrow, from the open window I heard Leo asking for permission to take photographs, the way Ma laughed before saying, 'Of course! Of course! Do you want to pull up a few carrots?' and Win-win clapping his hands and crying, 'I can show you! Let me show you, Leo Shushu!' and I had to stop because my knees had grown weak with some emotion I couldn't quite name for this man from Hong Kong who I'd just met, and who no doubt was leaving Xiamen soon.

Chapter 8
Leo

Pearl walked me to the bus stop again, but tonight she was quiet. Had I upset her in some way? I retraced the evening in my head, but came up with nothing. It had been a lovely evening in every way.

This caused me to realize that I hadn't thought of Lindsay since morning — a new record for me. I prodded at the wound by calling to the surface a memory of Lindsay singing along to 'Eternal Flame' in my old car, the one we picked out together and which I bought only because I wanted to please her. I sold the car almost immediately after we broke up; I had never liked it in the first place. She used to tap out the notes of the song on my left thigh like it was a piano as I drove. I waited for my eyes to smart, but to my surprise, they didn't. The ache was still there — would it always be there? — but it had lost its edge.

Grateful, I turned my attention back to Pearl, who was looking down at her folded hands as she walked. The dim light of the flickering street lamps made it impossible to read her expression.

'Thank you for dinner.' I held up the bulging bag of *longan* fruit her mother had insisted on giving me. 'I've even got dessert for later.'

She smiled a little, nodding.

We arrived at the bus stop. An older gentleman was sitting in the middle of the bench, smoking a cigarette, but he shuffled over when he saw us approaching. We nodded our thanks as we sat down beside him.

'Where are we going tomorrow?' I asked, hopeful this question would cheer her up.

She glanced at me, surprised. 'How long are you staying in Xiamen for?'

Was she looking forward to my leaving that much? I hid my hurt by taking out my phone and opening the calendar app. 'I was thinking of heading to Jiangxi next, maybe.' I hesitated. 'But you said we would go see the *tulou* together.'

At this, I saw her face light up again, and I wondered if I had read her wrong earlier. 'Do you still want to? We'll have to leave early in the morning; it's a long bus ride each way, four hours, but everybody says it's worth it.'

'I do want to, very much. I'll meet you anywhere. Just say when, and I'll be there.'

She blushed. 'You don't mean that.'

'I do.'

The sound of her laughter was so sweet. 'Alright, then let's meet at the ferry terminal tomorrow morning. Is 7:30 too early for you?'

'Not at all.' I was used to waking up early for work, and since breaking up with Lindsay I'd been waking up even earlier than before, sometimes around 5 a.m., sometimes even earlier, in time to catch the sunrise each morning. I took pictures of those, too, but their beauty was free of the baggage that sunsets carried. '7:30 is perfect.'

The bus screeched to a stop in front of our bench, and just as

I was about to blurt out my number, Pearl was telling me hers. It was so many digits, so many more than the 8-digit phone numbers that I was used to, but she repeated them as I climbed on the bus, and as I waved goodbye to her I repeated the string of numbers under my breath like my life depended on them.

The moment I sat down, I recited her number into my phone using the dictation function. To my chagrin, it came out as jibberish (*Lean would Joe are batch lean Joe Sam wood are?*). It took me a moment to see the problem: I was saying the numbers in Putonghua, the way Pearl said them to me, but on its current settings, my phone only recognized English.

Groaning, I frantically jammed the digits into my traitorous phone instead.

'Why did you come to Xiamen, Leo?'

We'd been on the bus for about two hours now, with another two ahead of us, and we'd talked about everything from movies (my favorite, *Once*, and her favorite, *Titanic*) to our mothers' best dishes (mine: carrot cake; hers: meatballs with water chestnut). Conversation had flowed easily; it felt as if we had known each other for much longer than a few days. Every now and then she took a picture to send to her mother. Sometimes she snapped a picture of the view of a building or a street sign as we rumbled past; sometimes she invited me to join her for a selfie.

'My heart was broken,' I said, simply, and although I intended this as a statement of fact, and not a call for sympathy, Pearl placed her hand on my forearm, and I could see in her expression that she understood.

'Shame on her,' she said softly.

I was touched. 'I think it's healing, a little.'

'Win-win's father broke my heart, over five years ago.' She

turned to look out the window, studying the scenery outside, although the view had been the same for over an hour: winding roads through a lush mountainous area. 'It was horrible. I thought my life was over.' She hesitated. 'But he got what he deserved, don't you think? He hasn't got to see Win-win grow up. He's missed everything.'

I marveled that Pearl considered herself the lucky one, even though the man got off scot-free, with no responsibilities whatsoever. I felt a great surge of—respect? warmth? love? I couldn't tell for certain—towards this woman. 'Definitely. Shame on him, too.'

She held up a fist as though it was a beer mug. 'Cheers to the broken-hearted.'

I bumped her fist with mine. 'Cheers.'

The *tulou* at Tianluokeng Village were odd-looking structures—stout and drum-like, with a hollow centre, the courtyard. They were enormous: according to Pearl, this one had a diameter of over 50 meters, and that one, over 60 meters. They looked like heavily fortified fortresses from the outside, but from the inside it was clear that they had once served as communal homes. 'For a clan of up to 800 people,' Pearl informed me, clearly enjoying how I impressed I was.

'This *tulou* has 32 rooms,' she continued proudly, as though the imposing structures were her personal masterpiece. I wondered what it would be like to live in a *tulou* with Mom and Dad, and Henry and Melissa, and Corrie, and all our relatives. The thought of it made me feel faint. I was Mom's favorite, and Grandma's, but this didn't stop them from breathing down my neck about being a bachelor at forty. And Melissa was always trying to tell me how to live my life—her frequent and unsolicited advice in the confines of a *tulou* would be hard to bear indeed. It'd be fun to see Corrie more often though, I thought, suddenly missing my little niece. She was a sassy one, Corrie, but a lot of fun. I'd have to remember to buy her a souvenir before the end of the summer.

Pearl coaxed me to pose with this gate, that wall. I did it to please her, but I had always felt self-conscious being in photographs by myself. 'Smile!' she ordered, giggling. 'Show more teeth!'

It was nearly 3 p.m. by the time we climbed on the bus to return to Xiamen. To my surprise, Pearl was quiet again, and I wondered once more if I had upset her. When I glanced at her, though, I saw that she had nodded off. The bus made a sharp turn, and her head lolled against me. She shifted in her seat a little, then continued resting her head on my shoulder. Part of me wondered why I wasn't pulling away. Was this too much too soon?

My breath caught as I glanced at Pearl. She was so very lovely, but not in the conventional way that people in Hong Kong often see beauty. She didn't have double-lidded, heavily made-up eyes framed with long, artificial lashes or pouty red lips, but I was drawn to the warmth of her smile, the way her eyes resembled a pair of crescent moons when she laughed, or like now, when she was asleep. Unlike Lindsay, Pearl wore very light make-up only. Her hair was black, and often tied up in a no-nonsense braid or ponytail. This was very different from Melissa, Lindsay, and even my mother, who loved spending hours at the salon and often sported a different color and hairstyle every month. There was something so wonderfully joyful about Pearl; even now, in her sleep, the corners of her mouth were upturned, as though she was dreaming about something good and sweet.

And yet, I mused, I was attracted to her not so much because of the way she looked — although with each passing day I was finding her more and more beautiful. I turned back to the window, and as we rumbled past hectare after hectare of verdant farmland, what I kept coming back to was her character. I'd never known anyone like her—confident, courageous, strong and self-sufficient. She was incredibly different from the stereotypical Hong Kong woman, who was loved because she was needy and helpless. All my life I had thought that was the way all women were.

But asleep on my shoulder was Pearl, a breath of fresh air, a snowy swan among a flock of preening ducks.

Chapter 9
Pearl

'Pearl, we're nearly here,' someone was saying. He smelled good, clean, like Dettol body wash. In my half-asleep state it took me a moment to realize it was Leo. I'd been asleep on his shoulder.

I sat up abruptly, suddenly shy. 'I'm sorry,' I murmured, rubbing my eyes. Glancing out the window, I could see that we were back in downtown Xiamen; the bus was just a few blocks from the terminus. Night had fallen during the time we were on the bus. 'Have I been asleep for long?'

When he smiled, I noticed—and not for the first time—that he had very kind eyes. 'You dozed off almost immediately after we got on the bus.' He glanced at his watch, shrugged. 'I guess around four and half hours.'

Instinctively, I reached out a hand and squeezed his shoulder, knowing it had to be numb from so many hours of inactivity. That's how it always was when Win-win fell asleep against me, and I was much heavier than Win-win.

He placed his hand over mine, stopping it. 'I'm fine,' he said, gently.

My gaze met his, and something passed between us,

something as palpable and electric as lightning.

I could love this man, I thought, my hands trembling. My heart was hammering in my chest and suddenly my cheeks felt so hot it was like I had a fever.

'May I hold your hand?' he asked hesitantly.

No one had ever asked me for permission to hold my hand. A long-forgotten memory of Hong—Hong, who had treated my body like it was nothing—surfaced, unbidden. I thought of how, on our first date, at a dirty cinema with stained seats, he had reached down the front of my blouse the moment the lights went out, how roughly he had fondled my breasts and though it had hurt I didn't dare move. He had thrust his tongue into my mouth, and how Hong's breath had always reeked—of garlic, of cigarettes. Sometimes, when I saw Hong's profile in Win-win's, I feel such a tension between regretting that part of my life and being intensely grateful for it, for without it there would be no Win-win.

I could see that Leo had mistaken my hesitation for rejection and was struggling to hide his disappointment. His smile was forced; his expression confused. But when I nodded, his face lit up again and he took my hand in his, gently, as though it was something very precious. I wished my hands would stop shaking. It was only when the bus screeched to a stop inside the terminus that he let go, briefly, to grab our bags from the overhead compartments before reaching for my hand again.

――――∾――――

I was leading Leo to the bus stop for the last leg of the journey home when he flagged down a taxi. 'Faster this way,' he said, opening the door and helping me inside. It seemed like the most natural thing in the world when he climbed in after me. I didn't tell him to go back and rest at the hotel; he didn't explain that he wanted to take me home.

The air-conditioning in the taxi was on full blast, and even though I was still sweating, I sneezed. Leo immediately pulled out a crumpled windbreaker from his backpack and draped it around me like a blanket. His hand hovered over my shoulder for a moment, waiting for my okay. When I nodded, he curled his arm around my shoulders so that my head could rest against him. I felt that same electricity coursing through my veins and I shivered, even though I was no longer cold.

My phone buzzed in my pocket. It was a picture of Win-win, an orange wedge in his mouth forming a silly smile. 'We're nearly home, little piglet,' I responded quietly in a voice message. 'Listen to what's on the radio.' I held the phone up so it was facing the speakers on the dashboard.

The driver turned up the volume for my benefit. It was a very old pop song that I grew up listening to, and which Ma still played on the stereo at home all the time. I recorded about ten seconds and sent it off to Win-win. 'Thank you, *shifu*,' I said to the driver. He gave us a grin in the rearview mirror before turning the volume back down.

'It's catchy,' Leo commented beside me. 'It isn't in Putonghua, is it?'

I shook my head. 'It's in the Min dialect. It's about—' I paused, trying to think of an accurate translation of the title. 'I guess it sort of means *if you want to win you have to fight for it*. Keep trying, don't give up, that sort of thing. Everybody knows it. You can ask my mom to sing it for you when we get home.' I giggled at Leo's widened eyes. 'Kidding.'

My phone buzzed again; it was a 10-second clip of Win-win singing the chorus from the same song. The driver chuckled as he drove. I responded with three kissy face emojis and slipped the phone back in my pocket.

'Have you ever been to Hong Kong?'

'Not yet. I'd love to visit, one day.'

'It's only about four hours away by high-speed rail, no longer than it took to get to the *tulou* today,' he said eagerly. 'I would love to show you around. You and Win-win both. He'd love Disneyland, and we've got a zoological and botanical garden, too, a little one, not big like the one here.'

I pretended to consider this. 'But does it have cactuses?'

As I hoped, Leo laughed. 'Come find out. How about sometime this summer? I don't need to be back at work until the end of August.'

I sat up, my heart thundering in my chest. Had he really just invited me to go to Hong Kong? We just met a few days ago.

'No pressure, of course,' he said hastily. I could almost see him taking a visible step back. 'I just—'

'Give me some time to think about it,' I said, squeezing his hand with all the tenderness that I felt for him and hoping desperately that he could sense it. The last thing I wanted to do was hurt him. 'I really want to, though.'

His expression softened. 'If you come, you could stay with me,' he said. 'I could be your guide this time.'

We got home just as Ma was toweling dry Win-win's hair in the bathroom. It stood up in spikes, hedgehog-like. Win-win ran over to us and hugged us both, as though he had done this all his life. And for a moment I allowed myself to wonder if maybe it wasn't such an impossibility, that maybe Win-win could have a daddy again one day, and that it would be a marvelous thing, wouldn't it, if that daddy were someone as good, as kind, as Leo.

A SUMMER LIKE THAT

As Leo and I walked, hand in hand, to the bus stop, I could feel tension between us — but the tension felt good. It was the kind of tension that made me think of science lessons from primary school. It was like the potential energy stored up in a stretched rubber band, which given the chance, could fly straight across a room. I thought about the way my hand fit in his, the way he asked me to go to Hong Kong with him. My heart felt like that stretched rubber band. How far could it fly?

'Pearl—'

'Leo—'

We laughed.

'You first,' we both said together, before dissolving into giggles again.

I gestured to him. *You go first.*

'I just wanted to say thank you,' Leo finally said, dabbing at the corner of his eyes with his sleeve. 'Spending time with you makes me so happy. In Hong Kong, sometimes I can be kind of serious.' He looked down at his folded hands, his expression bashful. 'But here — there are so many reasons to laugh, to be happy. I feel like another person.'

I tucked a lock of hair behind my ear as I sat down on the bench beside the bus stop. The stone was cool against my legs. 'Sit with me,' I said, patting the bench. I willed the bus not to come so soon. He sat down, leaving about two inches between us. 'Closer, please,' I heard myself saying, a slight tremor in my voice. Who was this reckless woman?

He scooted over, close enough for me to rest my head against his arm. I heard him draw in a quick breath. 'Oh, Pearl,' he murmured, reaching for my hand. 'Where have you been all my life?'

I felt my knees grow weak at these words. *Waiting for you,* I wanted to say, but it seemed too much too soon. From a distance,

I heard the bus making its way to the stop. It was a struggle to hide the disappointment in my voice. 'Your bus is here.'

He frowned at the approaching vehicle as though it had personally offended him. 'Is it okay if we...wait for the next one?'

I hid my smile. 'Of course.'

We shook our heads at the driver and he gave us a thumbs-up through the open window. He pulled the mostly-empty bus from the curb and we watched together as the tail-lights faded in the distance.

'Will you think some more about visiting Hong Kong with me?' he suddenly asked. 'My apartment isn't big or anything, but there's plenty of room for you and Win-win to stay with me. I know we haven't known each other very long, but I—'

'We'll come,' I blurted out. I felt light-headed—the way I felt at work if I hadn't slept well the night before and missed my lunch break, too. It was true—I wasn't a very good judge of character a few years back, but in my heart I knew that this was different. Leo was different. 'I...I know you'll took good care of us.'

He smiled so broadly, his happiness so apparent, that I knew I'd made the right decision.

———∽∞∽———

By the time Win-win was finally asleep, it was past 10pm. Ma and I camped out in front of the television watching *Meet Your Match* as usual. Tonight's first bachelor was 26 years old and quite handsome, I supposed, with fair skin, dazzlingly white teeth and that tousled hairstyle that Korean stars favor, but his rather beady eyes kept flitting this way and that, never making direct eye contact with Shiu Yeye or the ladies. Ma and I both agreed that he didn't look honest. Leo's eyes were nothing like that.

A SUMMER LIKE THAT

Our usual late-night snack of tea and peanuts was between us, but tonight there was a special treat, a heaping bowl of candied sweet potato, Ma's favorite. Leo saw me eyeing them at the market by the bus terminus, and when I came out from the washroom he held them out to me, a shy smile on his face.

'That man from Hong Kong has been here three times in three days,' Ma said. She was trying, and failing, to sound nonchalant. She took a small bite of her sweet potato, chewed on it thoughtfully. 'That's interesting, don't you think?'

Moments before falling asleep, Win-win said, groggily, 'Will Leo Shushu come tomorrow, too?' Ma wasn't the only one who'd noticed something going on.

I felt my cheeks growing hot. I took a small sip of tea, stalling.

'I don't think he knows anybody else in Xiamen,' I finally said.

'Silly child.' Ma rolled her eyes. 'He likes you. It's very obvious.'

Ma was right—things had progressed at breakneck speed in the past few days. Who was I kidding? I would love to see more of him. And spending a few days in Hong Kong with him as our guide sounded like a dream. I tried not to think about what would happen at the end of such a trip. We hadn't talked about that.

I kept my eyes fixed on the television. I was hoping to just watch *Meet Your Match*, mindlessly enjoying the dreamy love stories—authentic or contrived, who could tell for sure?—and save daydreaming, and worrying, about my own reality later, when I was safe in bed.

'...happiness is at stake. Not only yours, but Win-win's, too. You think chances like this come every day?' I realized that Ma has been speaking to me the whole time. She was careful to keep her voice down, no doubt to avoid waking Win-win, but the frustration in her voice was unmistakable. 'Leo is from Hong Kong, and if you married him—'

'Ma,' I protested, alarmed. 'We just met. You're talking like a crazy woman.'

'*You* are the crazy one for not seeing this as the golden opportunity that it is.' She glared at me as though I was a little girl being scolded for having misbehaved at school. I looked away. 'Leo is well-mannered, well-educated, and...from the sounds of it, reasonably well-to-do.'

'We don't talk about money,' I muttered, wishing Ma would stop talking as though I were some gold-digger, just waiting to reel in the proverbial golden turtle. I hated to think of myself that way, when I'd tried so hard to provide for my mother and son through honest work. And it was true—money wasn't a topic that had come up in our conversations. All I knew was that he worked as an English teacher and lived on his own.

'I mean, he's *reasonably* well-to-do, isn't he?' Ma continued, more gently. 'It isn't wrong to want to forge an easier path for Win-win, you know. And for yourself.'

'I definitely think he's a good man, but it isn't because he's from Hong Kong.' I stopped abruptly, my cheeks reddening. I hadn't meant to admit that I was interested in him at all, but in front of Ma I felt so exposed. She could often read my mind. 'It's because he's so sincere and kind to me, and to Win-win, too.'

Ma smiled, finally satisfied with this answer. Reaching for the remote control, she switched off the television.

She stood up, gathering the teacups and dishes onto the scratched plastic tray. She took her time, knowing I wasn't finished.

'Ma,' I suddenly blurted out, 'wait.'

I could tell she was hiding her smile as she set the tray back down and sat down beside me.

A SUMMER LIKE THAT

'You're right. There is something...something between us.'

A smile spread on Ma's face. 'Tell me more.'

I couldn't help but return her smile. 'He's invited me and Win-win to Hong Kong to visit him.'

She let out a great belly laugh. 'I knew it! I knew it from the start! And how very good of him to extend the invitation not only to you, but to Win, too.'

My expression grew serious. 'Do you think it's okay for us to go? I haven't told him yes, but I think it could be fun, for Win-win especially. Leo said he'd take us to Disneyland, Ma.'

'Sounds perfect.'

'He...also asked us to stay with him. He said we can have his bedroom, and he'll sleep in the living room.'

Ma glanced at me. 'How do you feel about that?'

'I—' I picked up a piece of candied sweet potato and ran my index finger along the ridges on its glossy orange surface as I tried to make sense of my thoughts. When Leo was with me, beside me, my mind was so full of him I could barely think straight. When he suggested that we stay with him, it seemed exciting and even full of romantic possibility. Now, though, back in the safety of our living room, it seemed incredibly reckless to bring my son to an unfamiliar city to stay in the apartment of a man we had met just a few days ago. It seemed almost unthinkable.

And yet I wanted to. I knew—I just *knew*—that Leo wasn't going to hurt us. Far from it. But even if it didn't work out, we could always come back. 'Hong Kong is only four hours away,' I said to Ma as much as I was saying it to myself. 'I...I think I want to, Ma. Just a short trip, a couple of days. Do you think it'll be okay?'

Ma nodded. 'My gut tells me that he's a good man. Of course, you should still be careful, keep track of your travel documents, that sort of thing.' She paused. 'But if everything seems good and right, don't play hard to get, Pearl. Think of the life Win-win could—'

I shook my head. 'We're talking about a couple of days in Hong Kong, not a lifetime—'

'I'm just telling you—'

'We're still getting to know each other, and—'

'But be open to the *possibility*, he may well ask—'

'Ma,' I interrupt, stopping her. 'Ma, I know.'

She squeezed my hand, her expression sheepish. 'Sorry. I'm just so excited. You deserve to be happy, you know. Leo could be your ticket to a brighter and more secure future.'

'Ma, I keep trying to tell you...I don't like him because he could take us to Hong Kong with him.'

'Sure, sure, you've got lots of nobler reasons, I'm sure.' she interrupted, smiling. 'It would be perfect, is all.' She picked up the tray again. 'I just want you to be happy.'

Win-win was normally an excellent sleeper, but around midnight, moments after I finally dozed off, I heard him whimpering beside me. At first I reached out a hand and tried to pat him back to sleep, but his whimpers grew louder, more insistent. In the weak glow of his Doraemon nightlight, I could see his head shaking this way and that, his arms thrashing wildly in the air, as though he was drowning. His eyes were screwed shut, his cheeks streaked with tears. 'Mama,' he suddenly cried. 'Mama!'

'Baby,' I murmured, shaking his shoulder gently. 'Wake up, baby. I'm right here. You're safe.'

His eyelids fluttered open. When he saw me, fresh tears filled his eyes. For several moments he just stared at me, and I began to feel frightened, too. What could have scared him so?

A SUMMER LIKE THAT

'Mama,' he finally said, his bottom lip trembling. 'In the dream you were very old and d-d-died and went somewhere very f-far away and I tried and tried t-to call you but you w-wouldn't pick up your phone, so I used a... a—' At a loss for words, he positioned his shaking hands in front of his mouth like a V.

'A megaphone,' I say softly, scooping him onto my lap and cradling him like he was a baby again.

'A megaphone,' he repeated, 'but you still couldn't hear me. You didn't answer and... and—' He buried his face into my shoulder, sobbing.

'I'm not going anywhere without you.' It was true. Hong Kong, Xiamen, anywhere—Win-win was staying with me.

His sniffles gradually died down and a few minutes later, they were replaced by snuffly snores.

———∞———

The next day, Win-win and I headed to the Public Security Bureau on Xinhua Road to apply for our two-way permits. We had never been in a government building before. I made sure we were both dressed respectably: I was wearing a knee-length collared dress, and Win-win was in navy trousers and a white shirt, both hand-me-downs, but freshly ironed.

I filled out the many forms as quickly as I could. Beside me, Win-win watched a Peppa video on my phone with the sound off. Every now and then he giggled.

'You're going for leisure, is that correct?' the officer asked as she checked through our documents. 'It is imperative that you state the reason truthfully.'

I felt sweat pooling in my armpits even though there was nothing to hide. 'Yes. It will be our first time visiting Hong Kong,' I said, gesturing at Win-win. 'We are going to Disneyland.'

This won a small smile from the stern-faced woman. 'You can

come pick up your permits in two weeks.'

On the bus ride home, I called Leo. 'Two weeks!' he exclaimed. 'That's too long! I was hoping to leave tomorrow, you know, and take you to Disneyland the day after that, and —' he sighed. 'Two weeks!'

I hid my smile even though he couldn't see me. 'Why don't you keep traveling without us in the meantime? Didn't you say you were headed for Jiangxi next?'

'I want to stay here with you,' he said, a pout in his voice.

Clearing my throat, I put on my best tour guide voice: 'As a matter of fact, sir, there's plenty more to see right here in Xiamen, including —'

'Pearl, I'm so happy you're coming,' he interrupted.

Beside me, Win-win was looking out the window, Wuwu perched on his shoulder. I suddenly thought of something I'd heard Shiu Yeye say on *Meet Your Match*, something about how life's purpose was *to love and be loved*. I closed my eyes, suddenly overcome by how very lucky I was. 'Me, too.'

Chapter 10
Leo

'Leo? Is that really you, son?'

'Yes, Mom, it's really me,' I teased, rolling my eyes at her shock at hearing my voice. In all fairness, though, it'd been weeks since I called them. I'd been in this room for a whole week, and I just informed the front desk I would be here two more. It'd begun to feel like home, although the style and color scheme — Muji-esque, all cream and beige tones — were so different from my apartment, which was mostly navy blue and grey.

'Are you...having fun? Where are you now? Henry called and said you were in Xiamen a few days ago, but—'

'I'm fine. I'm still in Xiamen.'

'Oh,' Mom hesitated. 'Is it... nice there?'

'Yes,' I said, thinking of Pearl flitting among the cactuses at the Botanical Garden, Pearl leaning girlishly against the rock wall of a *tulou* for a selfie. 'I don't think I've ever been anywhere so nice.'

'Oh,' Mom repeated, clearly at a loss for words. 'Are you... feeling better?'

I knew what she really meant — had I recovered from the

break-up—but I didn't want to discuss that just now. 'I'm alright, Mom. How are you and Dad?'

'We're fine. Your dad hasn't been sleeping that well lately, but apart from that we are well.' She paused again. 'When are you coming home?'

It was my turn to hesitate. 'I'm still traveling,' I said, vaguely. 'Maybe in a few weeks.'

I could almost see her furrowed brow. 'You've already been gone for nearly a month. Haven't you seen enough of China?'

I thought of Pearl, the weight of her head on my shoulder, of Win-win's sticky little hand in mine. 'There's still so much to see and do. I'll call you once I'm back, Mom. Promise.'

'Well, alright,' she said reluctantly. 'Leo…has…has Lindsay been in touch at all?'

'No.' She and Lindsay used to be very close. Mom already saw Lindsay as her *sunpo*, her daughter-in-law, was always preparing double-boiled soup with costly collagen-rich ingredients like fish maw and bird's nest. I considered telling Mom that her beloved Lindsay had been cheating on her son while still coming to dinner at their place—then decided against it. What would be the point?

'Oh,' she said. Well, send us a picture now and again, Leo. We miss you.'

'I'll send you a few right now. Mom, I have to go. Bye.'

I hung up before she could ask any more questions.

———∞———

'We should go sightseeing instead,' Pearl protested when I called later that afternoon to ask if I could visit. 'If you want to see Win-win, we can bring him along, if you'd like. You haven't even seen Xiamen University yet, and that's—'

'Can I please visit you first?' I asked again. I desperately hoped she would say yes. 'I can bring a snack for us. Don't tell Win-win, but I'll pick something up from McDonald's.'

In truth, I had a far better surprise for Win-win than chicken McNuggets.

'Okay,' she finally agreed. 'I just don't want you to waste your holiday on us.'

After stopping by the McDonald's across the street from my hotel, I loaded my surprise into the trunk of the taxi. I felt such a thrill inside me as the driver made his way towards Pearl's village. I couldn't remember feeling so excited in a very long time.

When I arrived at the mouth of the village, I could already see Win-win and Pearl sitting on the steps in front of their home, waiting for me. Win-win immediately jumped to his feet and started racing towards me. Pearl followed at a more leisurely pace behind him.

'Leo Shushu! Leo Shushu!'

He ran into my arms. 'I have a present for you, Win-win,' I said as I set him back down.

He eyed the unmarked cardboard box beside me curiously. It was quite a large box, about a meter tall and half a meter wide. 'That's for me?'

Behind Win-win, Pearl gave me a questioning look.

We watched together as Win-win ripped off the tape and slowly opened the top flap of the box. When he saw the red handlebars, the ones with the Spiderman design in the middle, he let out the greatest squeal I'd ever heard. He removed the rest of the plastic in a sort of dazed wonder. Taking out the scooter from the cardboard box with care, the sort that is rarely seen in such young children, he looked up at me, his eyes wide with disbelief. 'This is for me?' he repeated. 'For me?'

I grinned. 'It's all yours.'

He wrapped his arms around me as far as they would go. His head still burrowed in my belly, he said, 'Thank you, Leo Shushu.'

I nudged him towards the scooter. 'Go try it. See if it's fast.'

Win-win nodded, his eyes bright, then turned to his mother. 'Mama, may I please have it?'

Pearl cupped his face in her hand tenderly. 'You may.'

We watched him together, quiet, as Win-win mounted the scooter and zipped off on it, smooth as anything.

Pearl slipped her arm through mine and rested her head against me. 'Thank you so much,' she whispered. 'But you know,' she continued softly. 'You don't have to buy us things every time you visit. You're welcome here. *You*'re the best part.'

'Okay,' I agreed, kissing her on the forehead, although I had every intention of continuing to spoil them, both here and in Hong Kong.

In the glow of the afternoon sun, she looked lovelier than ever.

The two weeks passed by quickly.

At first, Pearl's mom was reluctant to allow me to help with the peanut harvest, but the third time I asked, she agreed to let me try. Loosening the soil with a trowel before gently yanking up the peanut plant so that the pods wouldn't fall off was tricky at first, but I soon got the hang of it and even won some approving nods from Pearl's mom and the other women in the village. I refused to wear a handkerchief like the women, but my scalp was smarting and peeling by the end of the first afternoon. The next morning, Pearl bought me a yellow and purple baseball cap with LAERKS emblazoned on the front to shield my head from the sun. Pearl tried to teach me a bit of the Min dialect, and I taught Win-win a few magic tricks. By the end of the first week, I could manage a few simple greetings, and Win-win could almost make a small handkerchief disappear.

There were moments when I wondered what exactly I was doing here in Xiamen. I tried not to think about what I was getting into — much as I loved Win-win, what would it be like to be in a long-distance relationship with a woman who had a little boy? How often would we be able to see each other? I forced myself not to think beyond their visit to Hong Kong. This pocket of time felt too good to be true, dream-like. I didn't want to spoil it.

I once read that people can hold more than one belief simultaneously — that is why we can watch a play and be deeply moved or frightened, say, by what happens, even when we know that it is all make-believe. I supposed that was why I somehow felt both content and confident that this budding relationship with Pearl and Win-win would continue to grow — and also felt anxious that this could not possibly last, and that I would eventually lose them both and be so heartbroken that there would be no hope left for me, ever. I didn't know how I could believe both — but I could.

Two weeks fully immersed in life here in the village have caused Hong Kong and the people in it to seem fuzzy and irrelevant. Lindsay, Mom and Dad, even the new school year looming on the horizon, just a few weeks away — I'd completely stopped thinking about them. What mattered was the peanut harvest, Win's coin and handkerchief tricks, and most of all, Pearl.

Last week, at my suggestion, we went to The F. Bakery for an afternoon tea of croissants and coffee. I had read their five-star reviews on Tripadvisor and was eager to take Pearl and Win-win for a special treat. We ordered dark chocolate and almond croissants for me and Pearl, and a coconut custard one for Win-win, as well as coffees and a babyccino for Win. When I went to the cashier to buy two dozen more to bring back to the village to share with the neighbors, Pearl had rushed over to stop me, her eyes wide at the expense. 'Don't buy so many, Leo,' she pleaded, gripping my forearm. 'They're so expensive. I don't want you to spend so much money on us.'

But I had insisted, and seeing Pearl's pride as she went door to door, sharing the goodies with her neighbors was well worth the cost. Afterwards, though, she had said again—'You don't need to keep buying things for us'—and I had wanted to protest, *But I want to spoil you. Please, just let me love you.*

I could see that even though Pearl's Ma didn't come right out and say it, she was pleased that I was courting her daughter. Towards the end of the two weeks, when Pearl announced that she and Win-win would be going on a trip to Hong Kong with me, her mother didn't ask any questions; she merely nodded. But I could see that she was hiding a smile.

On the high-speed rail journey to Hong Kong, Win-win read and re-read a battered comic book while Pearl and I talked in hushed tones. I loved to hear her talk. She was so funny and sometimes it was a struggle not to laugh out loud in the quiet train cabin, but her stories never poked fun at others, only herself. She made herself out to be an Amelia Bedelia-like character, someone always making faux pas and getting into trouble—at work, at home, among her friends. I loved the way she glanced at me, to see if I was listening, the way her cheeks grew pink with pleasure when I laughed.

Even when she was telling me about father, who lived in Shanghai with the wife and kids from his second marriage, her tone was light rather than bitter. 'He really needed a son,' she said, matter-of-fact. 'Ma always tells me that he loved us. Quite a lot, even. But he needed a son for the family line,' she repeated earnestly, as though to convince me. 'It wasn't his choice. He sends me and Ma gifts and things whenever he can.'

I didn't agree with this. I didn't like the sound of her father, a man who seemed cowardly and irresponsible, someone who was not accountable for the choices he'd made. Still, it was remarkable that Pearl's mother taught her not to hold a grudge against her father. As I watched Win-win I realized that I'd never heard Pearl speak negatively to Win-win about his father, either. I thought of my sister-in-law, who was always comparing Henry to Daddy Pig in the Peppa series to Corrie. My brother *could* look a bit silly when he got all pompous and self-important, but he was hardly a snorting, incompetent pig. I felt a sudden pang of sympathy for my brother.

As the train pulled into Futian Station, Pearl slipped her hand in mine. 'Only one stop left!'

I kissed her forehead, touched by her excitement. I dearly hoped Pearl and Win-win would have a good time in Hong Kong, and that they would only see the city's good side. About a decade ago it wasn't unheard of for Hong Kong people to discriminate against mainlanders, but those were different times. For the most part, local news agencies had stopped reporting on the parallel traders who bought baby formula in Hong Kong to resell for profit after they crossed the border back into the mainland. And anyway, Pearl and Win-win weren't going to offend anyone. They were tourists.

'Hong Kong West Kowloon,' a voice intoned over the loudspeakers. 'Next station, Hong Kong West Kowloon.'

'We're here, Win,' Pearl said to Win-win as I reached overhead for our bags. Pearl's mother had insisted that I bring some goodies back for my parents, so in addition to my carry-on suitcase and Pearl's duffel bag, there was a bulging plastic bag filled with carrots, peanuts, and a head of cauliflower. 'You ready?'

Win-win grabbed his toy turtle from his seat and hugged it to his chest. When I held out a hand to him, he immediately reached for it. Sensing his discomfort in the unfamiliar surroundings, I gave his hand two squeezes; he squeezed right back. Our train compartment was only about half-full, but there was still a great hubbub of activity as everyone hurried to gather their things and get off the train.

The customs officers had nothing to say to me, but they took their time checking through Pearl and Win-win's travel documents. I watched, anxious, from the other side. As I waited, I considered calling Mom and telling her I was back in Hong Kong, then decided against it. I wasn't sure how much I wanted to tell her about Pearl yet. The vegetables from Pearl's mom could go in the fridge for now.

The customs people waved Pearl and Win-win through eventually. Pearl looked overwhelmed, a sheen of sweat on her forehead.

'Everything okay?' I asked quietly.

'Sure. They were very thorough, is all. I've never had to say someone else's address in Cantonese. They looked suspicious.' She blew on her bangs. 'Anyway, turns out they understand Putonghua just fine. I told them your address again and they let us through.'

Win-win tugged on Pearl's sleeve. 'Mama,' he whispered. 'I need to pee.'

'I'll take him,' I offered. Pearl nodded gratefully. When she pecked me on the cheek, I felt ten feet tall.

A SUMMER LIKE THAT

'Oh Leo, it's beautiful,' Pearl said, her admiring expression matching Win-win's as I led them into my apartment. I hadn't realized that I missed it, but it was good to be back. It even smelled like home, like my peppermint aroma diffuser.

How thankful I was that I had my own place, and that I wasn't bringing Pearl and Win-win to my parents' flat. When I was a fresh graduate, only 10% was required for the down payment, so it took just three years to save up enough to move out of Mom and Dad's. As a secondary school teacher I could make my monthly mortgage payments, but only because I had chosen such a small flat out in the boonies. To cut expenses further, I went straight for the mountain view flats. Seaviews were an extravagance that I didn't really care for.

I had pored over interior design websites for months and finally settled on a color theme I knew I would never tire of: navy blue walls with grey furniture. Eight years later, I still liked the charcoal floor-to-ceiling bookshelves, the pale grey loveseat with its off-white cushions, the square glass dining table. I was relieved to see the cleaning woman had been coming regularly. My snake plant looked as healthy as ever.

As Pearl and Win-win washed their hands in the kitchen, I quickly scoured the flat for traces of Lindsay—the framed photographs on the piano, the charcoal sketches I had tacked on the wall behind my desk. In the early days she would sometimes sit cross-legged with a sketchbook on her lap, drawing my profile as I marked assignments. Before leaving for the mainland, I had kept everything as it was, hopeful that she might return, but today I stuffed all this into the back of my wardrobe without any hesitation.

When I returned to the living room, Win-win was sprawled on the rug and Pearl was taking out a tin of tea from her duffel bag.

JANE LO

'Can I make you some tea?' she asked, her expression demure. 'If you can just show me where you keep your teapot, I —'

    I took her hands in mine. 'You're my guest here,' I said. 'Let me serve you.'

Chapter 11
Pearl

I didn't want to admit it, not even to myself, but this luxurious home was making me feel rather insecure and out of place.

Leo told me many times on the journey to Hong Kong that his flat was tiny, just one bedroom, as though to preempt these feelings. And he was right—the flat *was* small, but it was also polished and refined, everything from the piano—an actual piano!—to the marble coffee table to the floor lamp with its grey glass lamp shade. Even though Leo had been away from home for nearly a month, everything was tidy and clean, as though it could welcome guests at any moment. The flat looked like one of those show flats I'd seen on home makeover shows. I didn't know anyone who lived like this.

I quietly concluded that he must be rich, far richer than he ever let on in Xiamen. He always dressed so casually when he was travelling, always a T-shirt and shorts combo, always sandals or battered looking running shoes. He never talked about money, but I could see now that he never needed to. That should have been my clue; Hong never talked about anything *but* money, and he was as poor and stingy as they came. Leo and I were from two entirely different worlds. I resolved not to let him buy me and Win-win things whenever I could help it — I didn't want him to feel like we were here looking for handouts.

I perched on the edge of Leo's sofa, a neat little loveseat that looked fit for a magazine cover. I hid my discomfort by focusing on the décor: in this corner there was a snake plant, the largest I'd ever seen, about a meter tall, and sitting on the piano was an ornate wooden metronome, something that looked like it could be an antique. Behind the grey sofa was a large framed black and white photograph of a grove of trees, the tiniest hint of sunlight bleeding through the treetops. The black and white picture really suited Leo somehow.

'This is so beautiful,' I said, gesturing at it. 'Did you take it?'

He nodded. 'I was in Malaysia with my brother.' He paused, thinking. 'I guess it must have been nearly ten years ago, a couple months before he got married. I took so many pictures, mostly rubbish, but I liked the way the light hit the trees in this one.' His expression was wistful. 'It felt hopeful.'

As Leo spoke he pulled out several bags of chips from his cupboard, and after carefully checking the expiry date on each bag, poured out a selection for us and set the bowls on the coffee table. His head disappeared into his refrigerator for several moments before he emerged with two juice boxes. Checking the expiry date and finding it acceptable, he placed them beside the chips. I felt so nervous about Win-win spilling things, but Leo kept telling us to make ourselves at home.

To my surprise, Win-win did seem to feel right at home here. A chip in each hand, he lay on his tummy on the shaggy rug in front of the flat screen television. He laughed, even though he didn't understand what the furry characters were saying; they were speaking in English. I'd seen televisions of this size only in department stores.

A SUMMER LIKE THAT

As Leo fixed us tea in his very modern open-concept kitchen — I could just hear Ma saying how impractical such a kitchen would be, all that oil and grease flying everywhere with no tiled walls to stop it — he sang along with the songs from the programme. I'd never heard him sing till now; his voice was deep and rich, his English beautiful. I wondered why he knew the words to these children's songs, then remembered that he had a niece about Win-win's age. I squirmed at the thought. Did Leo's family know about us? What would they think of us, two strangers from the mainland? I was almost certain that they would feel that I wasn't good enough for him. And they would be right, too. I was just a girl from a little village in Xiamen, not quite a teacher and not quite a tour guide...

I forced myself to focus on the programme on TV. Win-win surprised us both when he fell asleep on the rug halfway through. Leo scooped him up and carried him the short distance to his bedroom.

His room smelled of peppermint and something else — lavender? — and followed the same color scheme as the living room: navy sheets on the double bed, a grey wooden bedside table with a lamp whose glass shade matched the floor lamp outside, a pale grey wardrobe in the corner. Behind the bed was another framed black and white photograph, this one a sunset — or was it a sunrise? — overlooking Hong Kong. Memories of that night at Sunlight Rock, when Leo had been so heartbroken, came to mind, unbidden.

Leo lay Win-win down on the bed with such care that he did not stir at all. I sat down beside Leo and rested my head on his arm. I could feel his warmth through the fabric of his T-shirts, each rise and fall of his chest.

He picked up my hand and kissed it, the expression in his eyes tender. I tilted my chin up coyly towards him. His hand was on the small of my back then, drawing me close, and before I had quite closed my eyes, his lips were on mine. He was gentle, but not so gentle that I couldn't feel pleasure, sweet and urgent, pooling within me. I heard someone let out a gasp and realized it was me.

He pulled back slightly. 'Is this okay?' he whispered. 'Do you want to continue?'

Not trusting my voice, I nodded.

He led me back to the living room wordlessly. Unlike at home, where all the houses were built directly beside each other, with one living room window looking into the next, such that you could watch the news without turning on your own television set, Leo's view felt impossibly luxurious. Nothing but mountains, not another person in sight.

'Again, please,' I murmured, suddenly emboldened. 'Will you kiss me again?'

'Ma? Can you hear me?'

'Yes, but not very clearly. Your voice is very soft.' Ma lowered her voice. 'Is he treating you well?'

I'm curled up on Leo's loveseat, my head on his lap. He was stroking my hair; I liked the way his fingers felt on my head. It made me shiver all over. 'Yes, very well.'

'I can hear the happiness in your voice,' she said quietly, and I could hear the smile in hers. 'Have you already slept together?'

I blushed furiously. I was thankful she couldn't see me. 'Ma!' I protested. I reached up to touch Leo's lips, remembering. He grinned, kissed the pads of each finger so playfully that I had to bite back a giggle. 'Um, of course not.'

'Mmm,' she said, clearly unconvinced. 'How's Win-win?'

'Oh, he's well—but asleep. Tired after the train ride.'

'Yes, of course.' She hesitated. 'You're...safe, right?'

I curled up even closer to Leo. I felt safer than I'd ever felt in my life. 'Yes. Everything's fine. You be careful too, okay?'

'Sure. Take care then, daughter.'

'You too.'

When I hung up, I felt a small tug of homesickness. I'd send her a message later in the evening to make sure she remembered to lock the front door.

Leo glanced at me. 'Everything okay at home?'

'Sure.' I paused, then decided to be more honest. 'It's just that my mom hasn't lived alone in years. It's our first time away from home. She'll be fine, though,' I continued, to reassure myself as much as Leo. 'It's only for a couple of days.'

He took my hands in his. 'Hey, if you need to go back earlier than we planned, it's no problem. I —'

'Leo,' I interrupted softly, 'we just got here. I *want* to be here.'

After Win-win woke up, Leo suggested that we go out for dinner. 'Do you feel like noodles? Something soupy? There's a great noodle place nearby — about a ten-minute walk away.'

I nodded, and Win-win shrugged good-naturedly. 'You decide, Leo Shushu.'

'And we'll pass by a playground on the way,' Leo said eagerly. 'There's a swing set and a couple of slides. You want to check it out?'

'Yes!' Win-win cried, rushing to put on his shoes.

It was late evening by the time we left Leo's building. The air felt cooler than it did earlier in the day, and on our way to the restaurant, we passed by an abandoned ferry pier and a small, rocky beach. We'd missed the sunset, but the night-time view of Hong Kong's bridges was breathtaking in its own way. 'That's the Tsing Ma Bridge, Win,' Leo said, pointing out the prettiest and most brightly lit of the three bridges to Win-win. 'And that's Route 3 — the one closest to the airport.'

When we arrived at the promised playground, Win-win was delighted to find that there were no other children and he had the slides all to himself. Leo and I sat down on a bench and watched Win-win as he nimbly made his way to the top of the climbing frame before sliding down the tube slide, giggling the whole way down.

Leo squeezed my hand. ' I'm so happy you're here.'

I pecked him on the cheek. 'Me, too.'

He snuck a quick glance at Win-win, and, content that he was facing the other way, cupped my face in his hand and kissed me so tenderly I couldn't help but close my eyes. A part of me was afraid that Win would see us, but this voice of reason was quickly drowned out. I wished Leo would never stop.

'Mama!' On the edges of my consciousness I heard Win-win's voice. 'Can you push me?'

With some effort, I pulled away. It took me a moment to catch my breath before I was able to respond.

'I'll go,' Leo offered, standing up. He kissed the back of my hand, knight-like, before jogging over to the swing set. 'I'm coming, Win-win!'

From my spot on the bench, I took a short video of the two of them — Leo teaching Win how to keep his legs straight and curl them back at the right moments, and Win-win, his face scrunched up as he concentrated on following Leo's instructions — and sent it to Ma. She responded immediately with three characters, *fei chang hao*! Excellent!

A SUMMER LIKE THAT

I immediately felt at home in the restaurant Leo brought us to. It was a casual, friendly establishment with an open-air section covered by a striped canopy; the tables and chairs were all of the folding variety, and our fellow diners were wearing flip-flops and undershirts. Win-win and I didn't look out of place at all. If anything, we were slightly overdressed.

'Sham Tseng isn't really known for anything other than roast goose,' Leo told us as we sat down. 'It's basically the only reason anybody comes to this area. Most people go to the big restaurant down the street—Yu Kee—but this place is my favorite.'

A grey-haired server dressed in a stained polo shirt sauntered up to us, a notepad and a ballpen at the ready. He asked Leo, 'Roast goose *lai fun*?' as if it was the only item on the menu. He set down three sets of china rice bowls, teacups, and spoons on the table.

Leo nodded. 'Yes, please—half a roast goose to share, and a pot of lai fun.' He turned to us. 'What would you like to drink?' He pointed to the beverage section on the laminated menu taped to the table. 'They've got lemon tea, coffee, milk tea—just the usuals.'

We decided on milk teas for the adults and an Ovaltine for Win-win. While we were waiting, Leo rinsed off all our cups and bowls with hot tea using the provided orange melamine bowl. 'They aren't actually dirty,' Leo explained. 'It's just what the locals do—my mother always said that the dishwashers in the back leave the last step for us.' He gave Win the job of counting out six chopsticks for us from the metal chopstick stand, then proceeded to wash those too. Win-win and I wiped them off with Leo's peach-scented tissues.

Just as we were finishing these preparations, the server returned with a large white tureen of noodles and a plate of chopped roast goose, the deep brown skin glistening in the glare of the fluorescent lights above us. Beside the goose, the server set down a rice bowl half-filled with a translucent golden sauce. Win-win licked his lips. 'Enjoy, Leung Sir,' the server grunted. Hearing them call him 'Leung Sir' made me smile—he was such a regular that they knew he was a teacher. I realized then that roast goose with lai fun noodles was *not* the only item on the menu, just Leo's usual order.

Leo thanked him before dipping the goose leg in the sticky sauce so it was thoroughly coated. 'This plum sauce is amazing.' He set the leg in Win-win's bowl. 'See if you like it, Win. The skin is very crispy, almost like a McNugget.'

I wasn't surprised that this was one of Leo's favorite places. The goose was as tasty as he promised—the skin crispy and the meat tender—and the noodles were presented in a delicate and flavorful broth, generously topped with finely chopped spring onion. We all agreed that the plum sauce was the very soul of the meal; I had to stop Win-win from licking the syrupy, tangy sauce directly from the bowl.

But it wasn't just the food, it was also the energy of the place—locals enjoying hot, tasty food in their flip flops and threadbare T-shirts. There were industrial fans whirring in the corners and keeping my sweat at bay. Behind these enormous fans were tall air heaters with their electric cords wrapped around their dusty bases: this restaurant was prepared for every season, every kind of weather. The gruff servers were actually kind, and treated Leo with respect. And best of all, playing in the background were songs that I recognized, as though they'd picked tonight's playlist with me in mind. I sipped on my milk tea as Teresa Teng crooned about how the moon represented a lover's heart, my heart and my tummy full and warm.

Chapter 12
Leo

'I actually prefer the futon,' I said, unfolding it onto the living room floor and stretching an old fitted bedsheet onto it. Out of the corner of my eye I could see Pearl crossing her arms, a frown on her face. 'It's firmer, for one thing. The mattress on my bed? It's far too soft.' I hid my grin when Pearl raised an eyebrow. Lying down on the futon, I folded my hands beneath my head to form a pillow. 'Ah, this is the life.'

'Leo,' Pearl said quietly, 'let me and Win-win take the futon. You sleep in your own bed. Come on.' She tugged at my arm. 'You must miss your bed after so many weeks away. Win-win and me, we can sleep anywhere. Right, Win?'

Win-win nodded, eyeing the two of us curiously.

I closed my eyes and let out a few theatrical snores. I heard Win-win giggling. 'Sorry, guys. I'm already asleep. Maybe another time.'

I kept my eyes closed, and for a moment I wondered if Pearl was genuinely uncomfortable with sleeping in my bed. Finally, she said, resignedly, 'Win-win, say thank you.'

He did. Pearl sighed. 'Leo, thank you. Sorry for the trouble.'

'You're my guests,' I said, grinning as I opened my eyes. 'It's no trouble at all.'

―――∞―――

Later, after Win-win was asleep in my bedroom, Pearl and I sat at the dining table, peeling the tiny mandarin oranges we bought on our way back from the roast goose place. Between us was a pot of Iron Buddha tea, the tea leaves from Xiamen. 'You know what we need right now?'

Pearl added a fifth orange to our tower of peeled fruit. 'What?'

'Dessert. That would be the perfect end to a perfect day.'

'It's already perfect,' Pearl said, tucking a lock of hair behind her ear with her pinky so she wouldn't get juice in her hair. 'I keep thinking this is a dream.' She opened her mouth, as though she was about to say something more, but closed it again. 'It's already perfect,' she repeated.

But I wanted to make it even better. I glanced at my watch. 'I really, really want to,' I said, my mind made up. Would it be quicker to call an Uber or just catch a taxi downstairs? It was already nearly eleven.

'But aren't you tired? Stay with me,' she said so sweetly I nearly changed my mind.

I leaned in to kiss her on the cheek. 'I'm fine. I want you to try their taro sweet soup—you'll like it, I just know it.'

Finally, Pearl relented. 'I'll take a shower while you're out.'

―――∞―――

I was planning on taking a taxi to Maritime Square to get the desserts, but when I exited the lobby, a minibus was approaching, so I climbed on. Because it was so late already, there wasn't much traffic, and with only two passengers on board, the driver took some liberties with the speed limit. I arrived at the shopping mall in less than ten minutes.

On my way to the elevators, I passed by the avenue of jewelry shops on the ground level, all still open for business. There were so many jewelry stores, each selling very similar products, but with their own distinctive window displays. TSL had a nature theme going on with butterfly and floral motifs, while MaBelle, which appeared to be collaborating with Disney, had a glittery arctic display, 'Into the Unknown' playing faintly from within. I thought of Corrie in her gauzy princess dresses, and my thoughts turned to my own family. I really needed to call Henry, and Mom and Dad, but I found that I still didn't want to. I hadn't so much as opened my Whatsapp app since coming back to Hong Kong — the number of unread messages had become unmanageable, and I just couldn't handle them right now. I felt my shoulders tensing up. I forced myself to take a couple of deep breaths.

I turned my attention back to my surroundings. Lots of the smaller independent stores had closed in recent years to make way for these mega chains whose target clientele was tourists, mostly affluent tourists from the mainland. Some locals resented these changes, but I didn't feel very strongly about the issue. It was inevitable for a city to go through different seasons, wasn't it? About a decade ago fro-yo places were on every street corner; then they disappeared and made way for the bubble tea shops. Now it was jewelry shops.

Feeling reckless, I strode into Chow Tai Fook, one of the largest of the jewelry chains. I told myself I just wanted to take a look. I was cheerfully greeted and invited to sit down on one of the little cushioned stools they had in front of the display cabinets. Someone set down a paper cup of tea for me.

'How can we help you today, sir? Can I interest you in a pendant? A ring? A bracelet? We have a *fantastic* selection, suitable for all occasions, all ages —' I noticed that the silver tag pinned to the shop assistant's mint green blouse had no name, just a number: 10441.

'I'm looking for something for my girlfriend,' I said. 'But I haven't decided what to buy for her yet.'

'Kindly allow me to show you some of our latest designs,' 10441 said, eagerly sliding out a tray of diamond rings from the glass cabinet with practiced grace and setting it down noiselessly in front of me, her head bowed. She held out the flashiest of the rings, the one with the biggest diamond. 'This here is the Queen of Hearts. It's the ring the model is wearing.' The assistant gestured to the LED screen behind her; a bride was lying in the arms of her groom, her hand draped across his chest. She let out a dramatic little sigh. 'Isn't it spectacular?'

It was, it was — the diamond on the ring was at least one carat, maybe more, a dazzling heart-shaped stone on a braided gold band. When she placed it in my palm, I studied it closely, but while it was luxurious and impressive, it didn't feel right. I tried not to think about the engagement ring I had bought for Lindsay, which she never had a chance to see, not to mention wear — it had been heart-shaped, too, but on a plain platinum band.

Much as I already loved Pearl — it was too soon for a ring. I didn't want her to feel like I was rushing her into marriage; the last thing I wanted was to scare her away. I wasn't even sure if my own heart was ready; I hadn't given myself a chance to think about that. Right now, I just wanted to make her happy; I wanted that more than anything. 'I'm not looking to buy a ring today,' I finally said, returning it. 'Perhaps a pendant.'

'Of course, sir, of course — ' she swiftly replaced the tray of rings with one covered in diamond pendants.

In the glare of the shop's spotlights and against the black velvet of the tray, each diamond sparkled. My eyes traveled up and down each column, searching for the perfect pendant for

A SUMMER LIKE THAT

Pearl, but none of them seemed quite right. None of the pendants had that bubbly sweetness which was Pearl — these jewels felt gaudy somehow, too showy. Sweat was rolling down the sides of my face; glancing at my watch again, I could see it had already been twenty minutes since I left home. Perhaps I would have to come back another time. I didn't want to keep Pearl waiting.

But I probably wouldn't get another chance to slip out and buy her a gift. She and Win-win were only going to be here for a few nights, a week tops, and for the rest of the time I'd likely be with them at every moment. I dearly wanted to surprise her with a present, something to tell her that I treasured her. She kept telling me not to buy her and Win presents, as though she worried that I would think of her as a gold-digger, but that was ridiculous: I was no millionaire. I just wanted to spoil her.

'Sir, if these aren't quite to your liking, we also have pendants in different shapes and styles with other gemstones — emeralds, rubies, moissanite, pearls —' The shop assistant slid out another tray and placed it before me. 'Please take your time. Can I get you some more tea?'

I shook my head, studying the new selection closely. The one in the bottom left corner stood out to me immediately and I knew I had found what I was looking for: a little rose gold cactus inlaid with tiny diamonds. It immediately brought to mind our first day together at the Botanical Gardens; I smiled as I remembered the way Pearl had flitted about the cactuses like some kind of fairy in her white broderie dress. The pendant was on a rose gold chain; perfect.

'I'll take this one.' I said, replacing the pendant on its little hook and handing the shop assistant my credit card.

'Excellent choice, sir,' she said, beaming. She rapidly typed my name into the computer system. Her face broke into a broad smile. 'You are a VIP of our company, Mr. Leung,' she exclaimed.

'You have 442 rewards points in our system that can go towards your purchase today. You bought a diamond ring at our Langham Place branch in October last year—'

I scowled. That was the stupid heart-shaped ring I bought for Lindsay.

If the shop assistant noticed my expression, she ignored it. 'And there's a special promotion for VIPs this week—if you purchase a pendant and necklace set, as you are now doing, you can choose one of these discounted rings for 30% off.' Her colleague rushed over with a small tray of eight rings. 'There's never been a deal like this. *Truly* incredible savings.' She glanced at her computer screen again before picking up one of the rings. 'This one comes in size 56, the same as the one you bought last time in October. Shall I get the same size for you this time?'

I felt my cheeks growing warm. 'No.' Pearl's hands were smaller than Lindsay's. They were different in other ways, too— Pearl's were a bit rougher, as she helped out in her mother's fields, and while her nails were neatly trimmed and filed, she didn't wear nail polish. But all this was beside the point—I didn't want to buy a ring today. I had a feeling Pearl wouldn't like the idea of such a weighty gift, not so soon anyway. I shook my head. 'Just the pendant and the necklace, please.'

'Certainly,' she said, with a touch less enthusiasm than before. 'Oh, yes—would you like me to engrave anything on the back of the pendant? I can do that for you right away; it will only take a few minutes. Officially, the maximum is 15 characters, but—' her voice dropped to a whisper. 'I can fit 20 if you need me to.'

The minutes were ticking by, but I couldn't resist—I knew exactly what I wanted the shop assistant to engrave on the pendant.

A SUMMER LIKE THAT

As I was digging around for my keys in the pocket of my jeans, my wrists weighed down with the plastic bags of Chinese dessert, a voice piped up in my head: *You know, you'll never really understand Pearl. And she has no hope of understanding you, either.* But languages could be learned, I reasoned, inserting the key into the lock. I could take an online course in the Min dialect. Or Mandarin. Maybe both. I could sign up for a few courses tonight. I could get some learning apps, too; wasn't Duolingo supposed to be good for this kind of thing? The students at school were always learning Spanish or French on their iPads. The nagging voice wouldn't let go, though: *Idiot. It's not just the language. How well do you really know this woman? How could you have just brought her into your home like this?*

'Oh, shut up,' I said into the empty corridor. 'Just shut up.'

I turned the key and pushed the door open. Pearl was sitting cross-legged on the rug, a crochet project — from the looks of it, the beginnings of a turtle — in her hands. In the glow of the floor lamp, with her yarn and crochet hook in her hands, she looked almost magical, like a character from a Disney film. I very nearly blurted out, 'Honey, I'm home,' like in the movies.

'Sorry I took so long,' I said instead, kicking aside my flip-flops. Pearl rushed over to relieve me of the bags. 'You and Win-win okay?'

'We're fine,' she said, kissing me on the cheek. She gestured to my bedroom door, which was slightly ajar. 'Win's sleeping really well, and I was just crocheting a friend for Wuwu. You must've waited a long time,' she continued. 'You bought so many things. Thank you.'

'There *was* a bit of a wait,' I agreed, reddening. I *had* waited a long time, but it was for the engraving, not the dessert. 'I'm sorry I took so long.'

I laid out two placements on the coffee table and Pearl

arranged the desserts and spoons. Even though everything was just in Styrofoam containers and the spoons were plastic, it all looked very good. I ordered glutinous rice balls with a sesame filling in a sweet potato and ginger broth, a tofu custard topped with red beans and taro-flavored tapioca balls, a mango pudding with evaporated milk, and mango pancake. It was a lot of dessert for just the two of us, but I wanted Pearl to be able to try everything, and anyway, Win-win would enjoy the mango pancake as a bit of a desserty breakfast in the morning. That little boy was just like his mother; they both loved sweets.

We sat cross-legged, side by side, on the futon. For a few moments we just ate in comfortable silence. When I glanced at her to see if she was enjoying the desserts, I was surprised to see Pearl holding out a spoonful of tofu custard to my lips. 'Try it,' she said softly. 'It's good.'

And when she fed it to me we didn't break eye contact and suddenly she had set down the spoon on the coffee table and we were kissing. I heard someone let out a sigh as she curled up onto my lap and it might have been Pearl, but it might have been me. She tasted so sweet and good and right, I felt almost dizzy with desire for this woman in my arms.

I reached over and switched off the lamp.

―――∽∽―――

Later that night, when I was trying but failing to get comfortable using one of the square sofa cushions as a pillow, my bedroom door creaked open. I felt my body tense.

It was Pearl—without preamble, she climbed under my blanket and fit her body against mine, a little spoon against a big spoon. The futon was narrow—just two and a half feet—but we fit.

A wave of love for her crashed over me. But this wave was

matched by one that was even greater, a wave of fear: *What if I lose you, too?* I pressed my lips against the back of her head, trying to steady my breathing. 'Pearl,' I managed.

She rolled over so that she was facing me. She was so beautiful in this near darkness, her eyes fixed intently on mine. 'I'm here,' she said, softly. 'I'm here.'

She wrapped her arms around my body, her legs too, and held me so tight and so close that there was no room left for fear.

Chapter 13
Pearl

We had been in this taxi for twenty minutes, but with the air-conditioning broken, it felt like much longer than that. All three of us had fans wrapped around our necks on full blast — I had bought a nice green one for Leo in Xiamen before we left for Hong Kong, one that matched his sneakers — and the windows were rolled all the way down, but the air that hit our faces was warm and muggy. I wasn't crazy about the way I was beginning to smell, even though I had just showered that morning. I was grateful that Win-win was sitting between me and Leo.

'Where are we going, Leo Shushu? It's far.'

Win-win's voice had a hint of a whine to it, but a quick glance at Leo's face showed me that either he hadn't noticed or didn't mind. Leo asked me this morning if I wanted him to shave, and I had shaken my head, blushing. I reached over to stroke his cheek. It felt like warm sandpaper. I liked it. Leo leaned his cheek into my hand, which made me smile. We were headed for Disneyland, but Leo made me promise to keep it a surprise for Win-win.

'Wait and see,' he said lightly to Win-win. 'We're nearly there,

A SUMMER LIKE THAT

I promise.'

Win-win frowned. It wasn't quite a pout, but close. 'Mama, I'm hot.'

He certainly looked hot; his fringe was plastered to his forehead, his cheeks the shade of pink guava. What I wouldn't give for an ice-cold box of guava juice! The large carton, 375ml, not the small. I was salivating just thinking about the tart, fragrant juice. My thoughts of cold beverages were interrupted by weak strains of music coming through the open windows—familiar, dreamy music fit for fairy tales with happy endings. Suddenly, Leo sat up in his seat. 'We're here! Win-win, look!'

I looked out the window, too—up ahead was a large copper water fountain in the shape of a whale, a Mickey Mouse figure bouncing up and down on its back as though he was surfing. Surrounding the whale were other familiar characters—that one was Donald Duck, and this one, Minnie Mouse. It was as beautiful as all the bloggers promised.

For a moment Win-win was silent, his expression inscrutable. He stared at the fountain, at the tops of the attractions beyond the entrance that were beginning to come into view, his eyes wide and unbelieving. Then, without warning, he grabbed Leo's arm. 'Leo Shushu, we're going to Disneyland? *Right now?*'

Leo grinned. 'Yes. You're going to love it.'

Win-in turned to me, his eyes bright. 'Mama?'

I nodded: *It's true.* He looked so happy, I thought he might pass out.

Over Win-win's head, I mouthed *Thank you* to Leo.

He shrugged shyly, as though it were nothing.

But to us, it was everything.

———∞———

The entrance to Hong Kong Disneyland was very busy, but

it was a kind of organized chaos—people were mostly lining up and the lines were moving along steadily. There were lots of tourists from the mainland, like us, but also many local families lining up to go in. We looked like a family, too. I'd already sent Ma a picture of us at the main entrance, complete with a voice message from Win-win: 'Ah Meh, we are at Disneyland! Disneyland! *We are at Disneyland!*'

Smiling staff in summery khaki uniforms and caps checked our bags after we pushed past the turnstiles. To Win-win's great delight, one of the staff crouched in front of him and placed a large Mickey Mouse sticker on his T-shirt. 'Have a magical day,' she said in Putonghua.

'Thank you, *jiejie*,' he responded immediately, as I knew he would.

The lady smiled before giving him one more: 'This one is for your turtle friend,' she said, plastering a smaller sticker on Wuwu's shell.

I appreciated that this was excellent service, the start of our magical day here, but as Leo held my hand and led me onto bustling Main Street, part of me couldn't quite get past the turnstiles. I couldn't stop wondering how that woman could have known that Win-win was not a local child, but one from the mainland who needed to be spoken to in Putonghua.

Was it his clothes? I glanced uneasily at Win-win, who was dressed in his favorite outfit: well-worn cargo shorts, just a bit small, and his beloved sailor shirt, the blue stripes now faded. His sandals were new, at least—but the Nike logo on them was facing the wrong way. The direction of that check mark had never mattered to me, until now. Suddenly it seemed to matter a great deal.

I looked around me at the many other children bustling around us: everyone seemed to be in high-definition, brightly clad, with Disney characters emblazoned across not just their clothes but also their daypacks, their hair clips, their baseball caps, while Win-win seemed to look a bit faded and washed-out. I felt ashamed that I hadn't done better for my son. I should have bought him a new outfit for today. My eyes were smarting, but I didn't take out a tissue; I didn't want Leo or Win-win to notice.

When I looked down at my own outfit, a gauzy purple skirt that nearly reached my ankles and a sleeveless blouse with a Peter Pan collar, I felt both overdressed — everyone seemed to be in shorts or capris — and underdressed — why hadn't I painted my toenails if I was going to wear sandals? The sandals themselves seemed all wrong: my thick-heeled sandals with their adjustable straps looked clunky and frumpy. The women here seemed to favor slim Gladiator-style sandals with narrow straps, or forgo sandals altogether and wear canvas shoes instead. In truth, I had packed this outfit with some care, thinking that the broderie collar would look nice in photographs, but now I wished I had just worn a T-shirt and shorts, like everyone else. I looked stupid.

Where had Leo and Win gone? There they were — about twenty meters ahead of me, studying the rows of Disney merchandise hanging from a canopied stall on wheels. Leo was slipping a pair of Mickey Mouse ears on Win-win's head, and to my surprise, the effect was instantaneous and transformative. With the oversized ears on, he looked like any little boy enjoying a day at Disneyland. I watched as Leo picked up a second headband, this one with Minnie's ears and red bow, and paid for both with a $500 bill. I noted that he did not get very much change in return.

'I found your ears, Minnie,' he said, holding out the headband to me.

I inclined my head towards him, and he gently slipped the headband on, tucking my hair behind my ears as he did so. His hands on my shoulders, he steered me to the other side of the stall, where a small oval mirror was hanging on a hook. 'Look,' he said, smiling at me in the reflection. 'See how pretty you are.'

With Leo's stubbly cheek against mine, his expression so tender, I did catch a glimpse of how beautiful I was in his eyes. I smoothed out my skirt. It wasn't so bad.

The shop attendant volunteered to take a photograph of us. Win-win stuck his head between me and Leo, wrapping his arms around our shoulders so the three of us looked like peas in a pod.

'Say *MICKEY*!' she cried. We did.

At Disneyland there were lots of rides, but also lots of people, everybody having a good time. The lines were deceptively long; they looked short from the outside but once you got in one, you discovered that the line snaked around this pillar, that pole, and spilled you into three separate indoor spaces, all beautifully decorated, before finally leading to the ride itself.

It took us a long while before we were on our first ride — It's a Small World — but it was worth it to be inside that dark and cool building, a wonderful reprieve from the sweltering heat outside. We climbed onto the boat, and everyone took out their phones — I wasn't the only one mesmerized by all those little wooden people dancing and singing. I wanted to remember the magic of the moment, and share it with Ma, too.

As I rested my head against Leo's arm, I felt his kiss on the top of my head. 'Do you like it?' he whispered into my ear.

I was trying to think of a response that might come close to just how much I liked it — liked not just Disneyland, but this summer, this growing love I felt for Leo — when he pressed his lips lightly against mine and I stopped trying.

A SUMMER LIKE THAT

The rides were fun, my favorite so far being the Buzz Lightyear ride, what with Leo and Win-win giggling helplessly while competing for points, but that paled in comparison to the shows. Leo took us to see the Golden Mickeys first, and the show was so well done that I wanted to get in line to watch it a second time. But he steered me towards the Lion King show, promising that I would like it even more.

He was right. Win-win and I had watched the movie version before, but I was still caught off guard when Mufasa died to save his cub. Even the children in the audience, including my Win-win, sat in silence, their expressions sombre, when Mufasa collapsed to the ground. On one level I knew it was just a skilled performer, the sweeping music designed to tug at my heartstrings, the rocks and trees on the circular stage made of styrofoam and cardboard, but the tears came anyway. I would gladly die in Win-win's place, too. But how I would miss seeing him grow up!

Leo was quick to notice, quick to dab my cheeks dry with a tissue. The peach scent of the tissue brought me back to those early moments in Xiamen, before any of this. I glanced at Leo, who had one arm around Win-win's shoulders, and the other stretched out to wipe away my tears, and I was brought back to the safety of the present. This sadness I was feeling was make-believe; rather than feeling sad, I had every reason to be happy. What had I done to deserve such good fortune?

As we emerged from the dark theatre, I was momentarily blinded by the glare of the afternoon sun. The exit spilled us out onto an unfamiliar section of the park, behind one of the food courts. 'I need to go pee, Leo Shushu,' Win-win said, tugging at his arm.

Leo took his hand. 'Sure, there's a washroom over—'

JANE LO

Something blue barreled into Leo with such sudden force that it took me a moment to register that it was a little girl. She buried her head into Leo's stomach, her arms wrapped tightly around his waist.

Chapter 14
Leo

It was Corrie. Corrie dressed in one of her many princess outfits, this one a sparkly Elsa dress with a silver and blue cape that flew out behind her.

And if Corrie was here, then her parents couldn't be far behind. I couldn't believe it, but I really shouldn't have been so shocked—Henry and Melissa bought annual passes for Disneyland every year like so many middle-class parents in Hong Kong. Still, I hadn't expected to see them today, of all days. Despite the awkwardness of the situation, I was happy to see my niece. She was exceedingly precocious, knew far too much for her age from eavesdropping on grown-up conversations, but I loved her.

'Hello, Corrie.' I ruffled her hair, but just gently, careful not to mess up her braids. 'I've missed you, princess.'

She stopped burrowing her face into my T-shirt and looked up at me, her face the picture of pure adoration.

'Uncle Leo, I *told* Mommy I saw you back at the Buzz Lightyear ride, I told her and I told her, but she wouldn't believe me, she said you were in *China*, and I said *no*, Mommy, I *know* what Uncle

Leo looks—'

'Leo, it *is* you,' Melissa's unmistakable grating voice broke in. Bracing myself, I reluctantly turned to face her and my brother, who would no doubt chastise me for returning to Hong Kong without telling him. 'What are you doing with that silly fan around your neck?'

To my horror, standing beside Melissa was not Henry, but Lindsay. Her wavy waist-length hair had been cut short into a pixie style that made her look both haughty and vulnerable. Her ears were exposed, elf-like. What was she doing here?

As though Corrie could read my mind, she let go of me and skipped towards Lindsay, her expression triumphant. 'Kaima, I *told* you, didn't I, I wasn't imagining things—'

It was all I could do not to groan. Of course—Lindsay was Corrie's kaima, her godmother, her mother's best friend. I felt the brick path shifting and sliding dangerously beneath my feet. *Don't throw up*, I pleaded silently. I could almost hear my stomach churning, churning, the bile rising. I tried not to think about the chicken curry I'd shared with Pearl for lunch. I pressed my lips together so hard they hurt.

'I, well, I—' I swallowed hard, about to try again, when I heard Win-win saying something urgently in Min to Pearl. I whipped my head towards them, startled. I had forgotten that he and Pearl were standing beside me, I was so shocked to see Lindsay. I noticed that Pearl had removed the Minnie ears from her head, and Win-win's, too.

Pearl squeezed my forearm. 'We'll be right back,' she whispered.

I looked guiltily at Win-win. 'I'm so sorry, Win—let me take you—'

Pearl shook her head. 'No, stay. I need to use the restroom too. We'll be right back.'

A SUMMER LIKE THAT

There was an uncomfortable silence as we watched them walk away towards the bathrooms.

'Who are those people?' Corrie finally asked.

I hesitated. *One day, hopefully my wife and child,* I thought to myself. *But we haven't talked about that. Today, she's my girlfriend and her son, but...*

I realized the three of them were staring at me, waiting for an answer. I attempted to clear my throat. 'I met Pearl and her son in Xiamen.' This much was true. 'It's their first time at Disneyland.' Also true. 'I'll introduce you to them once they come back.'

'Are they mainlanders?' Melissa asked. She said *mainlanders* like it was an insult. Behind her I saw Lindsay nodding slightly, clearly puzzled. 'I didn't know you could speak Putonghua.'

I felt annoyance—or was it anger?—flaring up within me. Why did it matter, one way or another, whether I had friends who were mainlanders?

'I can, a bit. And anyway, Pearl can understand Cantonese. They're my friends.' I wanted to tell them that I was dating Pearl and that things were getting more serious by the day but I didn't know how to say it without sounding like I'd recklessly started a rebound relationship. That wasn't true at all. *Or was it?* The voice in my head was relentless. 'Good friends. I'm showing them around the city, and Disneyland seemed a good first stop,' I rambled on. 'I'm thinking maybe Stanley tomorrow, or the Peak—'

'How did you become friends so quickly?' Melissa insisted. '*Good* friends? And why,' she paused here, frowning, 'why was that woman touching you? You two aren't...?' She let her voice trail off, glancing at Lindsay.

'Thanks for your concern, Mel,' I said coolly. The last thing I wanted was for Mom and Dad to hear about my relationship with Pearl through Melissa. Her version would no doubt be filled with inaccuracies and fabrications—a nightmare. I would tell them myself, on my own terms. I stole a glance at Lindsay, wondering how she felt about all this, then looked away. She was texting someone on her phone. If she didn't give two shakes, why should I? Still, I felt the old hurt coming back.

Suddenly, as though she could tell I'd been watching her, she looked up. Her denim shorts were so tight, the phone barely fit when she tried to slip it back into her pocket. She smiled at me, and though I'd seen it a million times, had dreamt countless dreams which featured a smiling Lindsay, she looked oddly unfamiliar. It was the haircut. Or had she done her makeup differently? 'How've you been, Leo?'

'Fine,' I said, more brusquely than I intended. When she flinched at my harsh tone, I was dismayed to find I still cared. 'I've been okay,' I tried again, more gently. 'And you?' I was keenly aware that Melissa was watching as all this unfolded. She had handed her phone to Corrie, who was quietly coloring a picture on the screen with her index finger. Melissa had painted Corrie's nails to match her own.

Lindsay shrugged, a little half-hearted shrug. 'Alright, I guess.' She gave me the once over. 'You've lost weight,' she declared, 'and you need a shave.'

I wanted this conversation to end. At the same time, a part of me, the old me, was lapping up Lindsay's attention. I felt disgusted with myself. She had made zero contact with me since the break-up, and now she thought I needed a shave? I hardened my expression. 'I kind of prefer it this way now.'

Out of the corner of my eye I saw Pearl and Win-win slowly making their way back, Win-win skipping on the tiles. He seemed to be avoiding the red ones in a sort of game. When Pearl caught my eye and smiled, I felt the confusion, the panic, receding. I regained my composure, for the most part. Some introductions were in order.

I coughed. 'So, um, Pearl, Win-win—this is my niece, Corrie.' Here Corrie hastily switched off Melissa's phone and handed it back to her mother. 'And my sister-in-law, Melissa. And—' I swallowed hard. 'This is Lindsay, Corrie's godmother.' I couldn't tell if Pearl remembered this name—I thought I had mentioned it when telling her about our breakup, but couldn't be sure—and if she did, she kept her expression impassive. I cleared my throat, then cleared it again—perhaps I was coming down with something— before switching from Putonghua back to English. 'And, this is Pearl.' I placed my hand on Win-win's shoulder. 'And this here is Win-win, her son. They're from Xiamen.'

The women nodded at each other awkwardly.

'*Nihao*,' Win-win said brightly, breaking the uncomfortable silence. Pearl was gripping Win-win's hand quite tightly, but he was fine, and regarded everyone with his usual openness. He smiled at Melissa and Lindsay, then turned to smile at Corrie, too. She was just a little shorter than him. 'My name is Win-win. I'm four and half years old.' He held out one hand to her, politely, but she turned away.

'I don't know what he's saying,' Corrie protested, slipping her hand in mine. 'Why does he talk funny?'

'Win-win's not talking funny, Corrie,' I said. 'He's speaking Putonghua. Can you say hello to him?' When she didn't say anything I gave her little hand a squeeze. 'Go on, then.'

'Hello,' she finally said, uncertainly, in English. 'Hello, Win-win. I'm Cordelia.' She shook his hand, a slight grimace on her face.

'Hello, Cordelia,' he repeated gamely, trying his best to say her name correctly.

'You can call me Corrie,' she muttered.

'Well, see you guys around,' I said, rescuing him before

Corrie could ask him any questions. I crouched in front of Corrie, registering her pout. 'See you *so* soon, princess,' I said, giving her a quick hug. 'Come play one day next week, what do you say?'

'But Uncle *Leo*—'

Melissa frowned. 'Leo, you can't just—'

I made a show of checking my watch. 'Five already! We really have to get going. I'm dying to show them the Autopia ride. They'll like that, won't they, Corrie?'

She nodded miserably.

Before I turned around, I caught a glimpse of Melissa frantically typing a message on her phone, no doubt to report my misdeeds to her husband, or worse, my parents. Since marrying my brother, she had seen herself as my big sister, a bossy and domineering big sister who was responsible for keeping tabs on me and making regular reports to my parents. I had always just tried to keep the peace to avoid upsetting Henry, and Mom, too—she loved Melissa like a daughter. Lindsay was watching us, her expression inscrutable.

I tried very hard not to care. We broke into a trot.

'Autopia, Autopia! Here we come!' My voice sounded false to my ears but it was the best I could do.

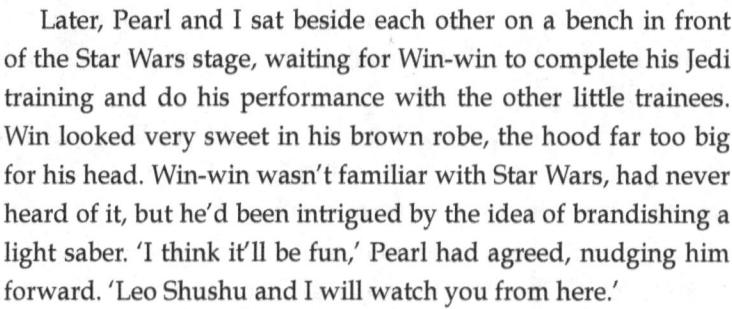

Later, Pearl and I sat beside each other on a bench in front of the Star Wars stage, waiting for Win-win to complete his Jedi training and do his performance with the other little trainees. Win looked very sweet in his brown robe, the hood far too big for his head. Win-win wasn't familiar with Star Wars, had never heard of it, but he'd been intrigued by the idea of brandishing a light saber. 'I think it'll be fun,' Pearl had agreed, nudging him forward. 'Leo Shushu and I will watch you from here.'

On the far left of the stage was Darth Vader, gearing up to be defeated by the children. We watched in silence as the children took their practice swings. Pearl suddenly placed her hand on my arm. Her touch had become so familiar, an anchor. But when I tried to take her hand in mine, she shook her head. She laced her fingers together on her lap, like she was praying. She was probably angry with me—I hadn't handled that nightmarish run-in just now very well.

We had both tried to keep cheerful and bubbly for Win-win's sake. The line-up for the Autopia ride was surprisingly short, so we went on it three times. Win-win rode with me twice and with Pearl once. They were supposedly race cars, but the ride was very slow, a meandering drive through a richly decorated path. Win-win loved it.

'I feel upset.' She was blinking rapidly as she said this, but a tear rolled down her cheek anyway.

'Pearl, I—'

'I feel upset,' she repeated, her bottom lip trembling.

I swallowed. 'I'm so sorry. I didn't know they—'

'That woman—Lindsay—she's the one who broke your heart, right?'

'Well, yes—'

'Why didn't you tell her that we are…we are—' She wiped a tear from her cheek with the heel of her hand.

I should have introduced her properly as my girlfriend, of course I should have. Why hadn't I? 'I'm sorry, baby,' I said, but it wasn't enough. 'I'm so sorry.'

I considered explaining that I had wanted to tell my parents myself about her, to not hear about us from Melissa…but I could see now that these were the excuses of a coward.

'Are you having second thoughts?' she finally said. 'It's okay if you are. It's just, for Win-win's sake, you know, I just don't want him to—' Her bottom lip trembled. 'You'd tell me, wouldn't you, if you'd changed your mind about us?'

I stared at her, finally understanding how deeply I had hurt her. 'Of course I'm not having second thoughts. I *love* you,' I said thickly, and though I was a grown man, just a few weeks shy of forty years old, I was in tears myself. I buried my face in my hands. How could I have treated Pearl like that?

With a start, I realized that she was squeezing my arm. 'Hey,' she was saying, her tone both urgent and gentle. 'Leo, please. It's okay, it's okay—'

Ashamed that the tables had turned and she was now comforting me, I forced myself to get a hold of myself. 'I'm so sorry,' I repeated, my eyes downcast. 'I'm so very sorry. I should've told Lindsay and Melissa just now. I'm such a coward, I've always been one—'

She tucked her hand into mine. 'No, you're not. It's okay—'

'No, I really should've told them. I can't believe I didn't tell them—'

'Told them what?' I was surprised when Pearl asked me this in a pouty voice—it was the first time I'd heard her use it, and it made me smile. I realized that she was jutting out her bottom lip, and it was an act. She was trying to cheer me up.

I couldn't resist. Gently, I cupped her chin in my palm and tilted it up so I was looking directly into her red-rimmed eyes. 'I was going to tell them that I met the most beautiful woman in the world, someone stronger and kinder than they could ever hope to be, and that I am desperately in love with her. Shall I tell them that, Pearl?'

'Well,' she began, a smile playing on her lips, but then suddenly she was on her feet, pointing at the stage. 'Win-win!' He was at the front of his line, ready for his moment of glory.

In her excitement, she fumbled with her phone, dropping it. 'Oh no, oh no, oh no-'

A SUMMER LIKE THAT

'It's okay, it's okay, I got this,' I muttered, barely managing to pull out my phone and start recording. I held my breath as Winwin sliced his light saber through the air, and struck Darth Vader in the chest, to wild applause.

Chapter 15
Pearl

We decided that Dumbo was going to be our last ride before dinner. Win-win and I climbed into one elephant, and Leo scrambled to get into the one in front of ours. As the ride attendant checked to ensure that everyone had buckled their seat belts, Leo took the opportunity to take pictures of us. I pulled Win-win onto my lap and we posed with matching peace signs. When I pointed my phone at Leo, telling him to smile for a picture, too, he blew me a kiss. I caught it and pretended to slip it into my purse, which made him smile.

A bell rang, and a cheerful voice over the amplifier cried: 'Dumbo the Flying Elephant is going *up* in the *air! Here we go!*'

Win-win's laughter matched mine as we soared higher and higher up, then plunged down low, dangerously close to the ground, before rising in the air again. With the sun just beginning to set, the sky a dappled mix of purples and oranges, Win-win's sticky hand in mine, and a lovely view of the wind in Leo's hair, Dumbo was turning out to be my favorite ride.

It was a beautiful end to what had been a beautiful day, but my mind kept returning to that uncomfortable encounter with

Leo's ex-girlfriend, niece, and sister-in-law. I wasn't planning on bringing it up again—it was clear to me how guilty Leo felt about not speaking up for me, there was no question about that—but the discomfort of sharing that space with them, and not being acknowledged, had hurt. The effortless way that Lindsay swung her Louis Vuitton handbag over her shoulder, the way she eyed me and Win with thinly veiled suspicion and contempt. Did he still have feelings for that Lindsay? She looked pretty enough to be a model.

Don't play hard to get. Don't make up problems where there aren't any. Ma's voice rang in my ears, frantic and disapproving. *You might not get another chance like this, maybe not ever. He loves you!*

But I was afraid.

I thought back to the day when I met Leo—how heartbroken he'd been, how much of a shell he'd seemed, hollow. How quickly we had connected after that—but was it because I was available, I was there? It was hardly an auspicious start to a long-lasting relationship. My cheeks burned as I wondered whether I *had* been taking advantage of him—even though I had never asked for any of it, he was always spoiling us with treats and surprises, and covering all the costs of everything. The tickets to Disneyland today would have come to nearly $2,000—more than half a month's salary for me as a teaching assistant at the kindergarten. I had a fleeting, terrifying vision of myself in a few months' time, unemployed, fully dependent on Leo to navigate this confusing, unfamiliar city. Would he tire of us? How could he not?

But I didn't ask for him to provide for me, I reasoned, as our elephant plunged to the ground once more. That much was true. *But you haven't stopped him, either.*

Afterwards, we headed to a food court disguised as a royal banquet hall, where Leo ordered chicken nuggets, burgers, and milkshakes for us. The nuggets were Mickey-shaped, which pleased Win-win to no end. Win-win dipped each nugget so far into the plastic tub of sweet and sour sauce that they were completely submerged in the yellow goop.

There was courtly music playing in the background that suited the regal surroundings, and even the servers were dressed in pretty Victorian style dresses with frilly aprons. Leo had his arms around us, the smile on his face one of contentment. I had every reason to be happy, so happy, and so did Win-win. But what was going to happen at the end of our visit in Hong Kong? Would that be the end of us?

When Leo inserted a paper straw into one of the milkshakes and brought it to my lips, I took a long sip. It was a chocolate milkshake, too sweet for me, but I pretended to like it.

There was time before the fireworks to stop at one of the many gift shops to choose a souvenir for Ma. Win-win and I looked at everything: the giant wall of plush dolls, the ones on the top shelf nearly as tall as Win-win; the spectacular array of girls' hair accessories, from oversized bows with polka dots and velvety hair ties to headbands like the ones we were wearing; the ceramic mugs, tumblers, and Thermoses; a sprawling stationery section; keychains and bits and bobs of every sort.

We finally settled on a broad-brimmed sun hat for Ma. I smiled at the thought of this loud Minnie Mouse hat sitting on my sensible mother's head. I hoped she'd find it useful in the fields, a nice change from tying up her hair with a scarf.

Win-win looked at everything quietly, stroking the stuffed animals with care, but didn't ask for anything. He held the brim of Ma's hat with both hands as we stood in line together.

'Would you like to choose something, Win-win?' Leo asked. We were surrounded by a dizzying number of children with armfuls of toys and trinkets.

A SUMMER LIKE THAT

'No, thank you.' He plopped the hat on his head, and looked at himself in the mirror, but the hat was so big it covered his eyes. I adjusted it a bit so it was balancing precariously on his forehead. We giggled as Leo snapped a picture of us for Ma.

'He's so different from Corrie, who's exactly like her mom — can't enter a shop without leaving with something, anything. She's a shopaholic already, and she's only six!'

Leo meant this as a compliment, but I felt a pang of shame that I'd never had the means to spoil Win-win like that. 'Let me buy this for your mom,' Leo continued, taking out his wallet. 'And Win-win, go — '

But I placed one hand over Leo's lips before he could say anything else. I kept it there as I spoke. 'Win-win, go choose something for yourself. Something nice.' I patted my purse reassuringly. 'We have money.'

Win-win blinked at me. I couldn't remember the last time I'd said that to him. Perhaps never. I nudged him forward with my hip. 'Go on, then, baby.'

He didn't need to be told a third time. Squealing, he sprinted towards the stuffed animals. 'Sorry,' I murmured, turning to Leo. 'That was rude of me.' But when I tried to remove my hand from his mouth, he reached for my wrist, anchoring it. He brushed my fingertips with his lips, and perhaps it was just my emotions running high but this struck me as incredibly erotic. 'Hey,' I protested weakly. 'Hey.'

He kissed me lightly on the lips, his expression penitent. 'I shouldn't have butted in,' he said. 'I should've asked you first. I'm sorry.'

I shook my head, my head whirling. Having a serious conversation about finances and boundaries seemed impossible just then. Out of the corner of my eye I could see Win-win stroking the purple mane of the donkey from Winnie-the Pooh.

'I'm not mad. It's just—' He looked so guilty that I couldn't resist cupping his face with my hands and kissing him on the ridge of his nose, right between his eyes. This caught him by surprise and he let out a little laugh which made my heart flutter some more.

I took a deep breath before trying again. 'You've been so kind to us. I'm just—'

I didn't have the words to tell him how loved, how spoiled I'd felt since coming to Hong Kong. I didn't feel like I deserved this happiness. I felt like Cinderella, happy like I'd never been before, but also acutely aware that this was a dream, and that time was running out. I almost felt as though spending Leo's money would accelerate that process and we would wear out our welcome faster. 'I'm afraid of what's going to happen when we have to go home.'

'We'll find a way,' he said, softly. 'Don't give up on us yet.'

The moment suddenly felt so tense I felt my eyes smarting. With great effort I channeled this emotion into a laugh instead, a nervous shudder of a laugh. 'I'm so thankful, I just—'

Leo stopped me from rambling on by kissing me on the mouth. 'Stop,' he murmured. I felt his arms around me, his hands stroking my back with a tenderness that made me ache with desire. 'It's okay. It's going to work out.'

Win-win ran back to us, a small Simba doll in his hand, and we made room for him between us. 'I want this one please, Mama,' he said, holding up the little lion cub to us. 'Is it okay?'

What happened next was completely out of character for me: I handed Ma's sun hat to Leo, took Win-win by the shoulders, and led him back to the wall of plushies. I grabbed the biggest Simba I could reach, a glossy two-foot lion cub with a long winding tail that ended in a fluffy brown ball of fur. Win-win stared at me, his eyes round. 'Mama...?'

A SUMMER LIKE THAT

'Yours is nice. But this one seems more...life-like. Don't you think so?'

Without speaking, he set his Simba back on the shelf and reverently took the one I was holding out to him. He'd never had a toy like this before. He buried his head into the lion's back. A moment later, he resurfaced, a goofy grin on his face. 'Yes, Mama.'

It took us ages to get out of the park after the fireworks. We were swept along in a sea of exhausted families, everyone slowly trudging towards the exits.

The three of us sat down on one of the wooden benches, Win-win resting his head against my arm. He was humming the theme song from the fireworks show, Simba in his lap, Wuwu perched on Simba's back.

Leo's arm was draped around my shoulders, but his eyes were glued to his phone screen, tracking the location of the Uber. His phone suddenly buzzed loudly in his hand. He groaned the moment he saw the picture flashing on the screen, a spectacled man of about seventy with a little girl I recognized—Corrie—in his arms. *DAD*, it said across the bottom. *DAD*.

Leo stared helplessly at his phone as it continued to vibrate. In the stillness of the night, the buzzing was very loud. It reminded me of the cicadas in our village.

'Leo Shushu,' Win-win finally said, tugging at his sleeve. 'Someone's calling you.'

Chapter 16
Leo

The last thing I wanted to do was pick up my father's call, but with Win-win pulling on my sleeve and Pearl watching me, concerned, there seemed to be no choice. I braced myself as I swiped across the bottom of the screen. If it were my mom calling, I would hold the phone a few inches from my ear, but Dad was less likely to shout.

'Hi, Dad.'

'So you *are* back!' he exclaimed. 'Melissa called your mother this afternoon, said she and Corrie bumped into you at Disneyland.'

Typical Melissa behavior. 'Yeah, I just got back yesterday.'

'You really should've called,' he continued. I could almost see his index finger in the air, reprimanding me. 'Your mother's been, what is it, trying to give you space, after what happened with Lindsay. But she was really hurt, you know, when she found out you didn't bother to let us know that you're back in Hong Kong. She's missed you.'

'I just got back yesterday,' I repeated, struggling to keep my voice level. Pearl glanced up at me from her phone; she and Win-win were looking at pictures from the day together. I cleared my throat, forcing myself to be calm for her and Win-win's sake. 'Sorry, Dad. I was going to call you today.'

Dad sighed dramatically. 'Do you want to talk to her yourself?'

No, I wanted to say, *not in the least.* Instead, I muttered, 'Yes, thanks.'

A loud sniffle, then, 'Son?'

'Hi, Mom. I'm sorry I didn't call. That was inconsiderate of me.'

'I'm not angry,' she said, in a tone that was decidedly angry. 'I've just been so worried, you know. I didn't dare call you when you were traveling, I knew how heartbroken you were, but truth be told I've been worried *sick*. You know how you can be, and in mainland China, with no one to protect you, who knows if some opportunistic woman might try and—'

'Mom,' I interrupted loudly. 'Don't get yourself all worked up like this. It's not good for your hypertension.'

Just then, our Uber finally pulled to a stop in front of our bench. I made a conscious effort to relax my features into a smile before gesturing to Pearl and Win-win to get in first. 'Mom, I have to go. The Uber's here. I'll call you tomorrow, okay?'

'Melissa said you were with a woman and her child,' Mom suddenly cried, accusatory, as though this were the trump card she had been waiting to play. '*Were* you?'

I watched as Pearl climbed gracefully into our ride, a grey Toyota Alphard. A moment later she popped her head back out, held out an *OK?* with her thumb and index finger forming an O. I responded with my own *OK*, even though I was far from okay. She smiled at me, that winsome smile I'd come to love so much, before disappearing back into the vehicle. 'Yes, I was.'

'Who were they, then? Friends from the mainland, as Melissa said? Or are you *actually* dating the first mainland—'

JANE LO

'My ride is here, Mom.' I said this as gently as I could, although I was furious. 'I'll call you soon.'

I hung up before she could respond and climbed in beside Win-win, who Pearl had already buckled into the middle seat. His eyes were already drooping shut. Seeing them made me stop wanting to slam the door shut.

Chapter 17
Pearl

Our Uber driver was surprisingly attentive: he handed me and Leo bottles of mineral water and switched off the radio right away when he saw Win-win yawning. Win-win nodded off as we pulled onto the highway.

I couldn't make out much of what Leo had said to his parents just now—he had spoken very fast, and in a confusing mix of English and Cantonese. It was obvious that he wasn't happy to be speaking with them—I had never heard him use that tone before—clipped and formal, completely at odds with the easygoing Leo I had come to know. I gnawed on my bottom lip, worrying, not for the first time, that there was going to be trouble ahead. Perhaps the trouble had already started. Was it worth it for Leo to bring this trouble on himself because of me?

'I love you.' Leo said this suddenly, fiercely, as though someone had been trying to contest this. He spoke with such depth of feeling, such conviction, that I felt a twinge of fear. What if things didn't work out between us? Could he bear it? Could I?

As we drove past a street lamp, I saw a tear glisten at the corner of his right eye; I brushed it away with my thumb.

JANE LO

Suddenly, I was afraid I was out of my depth.

———∞———

Later that night, when Win-win was asleep and Leo was in the shower, I curled up on the sofa and called Ma.

'Ma,' I said, all prepared to tell her about our big day at Disneyland. To my surprise, though, my voice was unsteady. I hugged one of Leo's sofa cushions to my chest, willing myself to be calm. 'Ma, it's me.'

'I know,' she said, gently. 'Are you having a good time?'

'Yes. I need to ask you something,' I try again, swallowing the lump in my throat. 'I'm not sure where this is going.'

'What do you mean?'

'He loves me, me and Win-win both. And I feel the same way about him…but we haven't talked about what's going to happen after we go home. I'm afraid that this isn't going to last. And if it isn't going to last, what are we even—'

'Do you want it to last?'

I hesitated. 'I don't think I deserve all this. It's like a dream. Almost like I got to switch lives with someone—' I tried not to think of Lindsay—beautiful, stylish Lindsay—and the way she had looked at me and Win, as though we were nothing. She had looked and even smelled rich with her no-doubt luxury perfume. A woman like that wouldn't need to be financially dependent on Leo, surely.

'Silly girl,' she said, and in that moment I could almost feel the warmth of her hand on my arm. 'How can you say that? You deserve every happiness in the world. Just think…if things work out, you and Win-win could have a fresh start in Hong Kong. Win could go to school in Hong Kong! Wouldn't that be nice? He could learn Cantonese, and English, and—'

'But he can't speak Cantonese *yet*. He doesn't know anybody here. And what about my job?'

'What *about* your job?'

'I'd have to resign, wouldn't I—'

'You'll have no trouble finding another job. Win-win will have no trouble learning the language and making friends. New beginnings for all of you.'

I considered telling her that from the little snatches of research that I'd done on my phone, I'd learned that it was illegal for me to work in Hong Kong on a two-way permit. It would take years for me to be granted a one-way permit and with it, all its privileges, including the right of employment. But it wasn't just work that was worrying me. 'Moving to Hong Kong would mean that we only get to see you a few times a year. How can we leave you, Ma?' I felt a sob rising in my throat.

I could almost see her shaking her head. 'We would only be four hours apart. I'd blink, and you'd be home. You'd be here beside me, helping me with the peanut harvest.' Without waiting for me to respond, she continued: 'How is Win-win liking Hong Kong? What did he think of Disneyland?'

By the time it was my turn for a shower, I had mostly calmed down. I liked everything about Leo's bathroom: the pebbly grey floor of the shower, the strange silver square that was attached to the ceiling and brought forth a rain-like downpour, and even the shower curtain, with its sophisticated black and white marble design. On the ledge of the frosted window was a reed diffuser whose fragrance I couldn't quite identify, but it reminded me of freshly washed clothes. It was very different from our bathroom back home, a dark little room with cracked tiles and that stubborn mildew smell.

The water was wonderfully hot, the jets of water that struck my back and shoulders sharp and strong. I breathed in the mingled scents of Dettol body washed and peppermint shampoo with pleasure. Just as at home, though, I was mindful of the water bill, and kept my shower short.

Coming out of the bathroom, I saw Leo sprawled on the sofa, reading a book in the soft glow of the floor lamp. I felt that low thrum of desire in the pit of my belly. Before I really knew what I was doing, I was going to him, kneeling beside him on the shaggy rug.

He set down his book on the coffee table. In the stillness, I could hear his breathing. I had the disorienting sensation that I was seeing a double image, one stacked on top of another, like film that had been exposed twice. It was as if I was seeing this man for the very first time—there was a little mole on his right cheekbone; his hair was not black, but a very, very dark brown—and falling in love with him again, anew. But at the same time, I couldn't shake the certainty that this man was *home*, that I belonged here, and I had loved him all my life. I set aside my doubts, my fears, and—

The lamp went out with a muted click. And as though this was the visual cue my body has been waiting for, aching for, it came alive of its own accord.

Chapter 18
Leo

I tucked Pearl in beside Win-win, who was sound asleep, the blanket still wrapped snugly around his shoulders.

'Don't go,' she said, her eyes already drooping shut. She had her hands folded under her cheek, like a princess in a story book.

'I love you,' I whispered into her ear. She responded with something unintelligible.

I switched off the bedside lamp and shut the door quietly behind me.

———∞———

Crawling onto the futon, I allowed myself to feel, for the first time all day, the ache in my lower back, the soreness in my calves. But although my body was tired, my mind was racing. I didn't think it was possible to fall even more deeply in love with Pearl…but I had. We hadn't talked about the future—both of us seemed to be avoiding it—and I was ashamed of myself for not having the courage to bring it up yet.

What would a life together look like? They would come to Hong Kong on two-way, then one-way permits, and live here with me. It would be marvelous to build a life together, if Pearl were willing...just thinking of having a family to love and care for made my heart hammer in my chest. It was something I'd wanted all my life, but had never dared to articulate even to myself.

We would have to make changes to the apartment so everyone would be comfortable, but I could buy a little loft bed for Win, maybe, or a transformer-type bed that pulled down from the wall, whichever Pearl thought was best. And we could change the curtains so they weren't so dark and moody — perhaps Pearl would like a floral design —

These happy thoughts were rudely interrupted by my mother's voice: *Who are they, then? Friends from the mainland, as Melissa said? Or did you actually decide to date the first mainland woman you met?*

So what if I did, I wanted to retort, so what if I did. What did it matter where a woman was from, if she was kind, and strong, and full of light? Wasn't it enough that I loved her, and she loved me back?

Although the air-conditioning was on, it was getting too warm. I threw off the blankets and rolled onto my side, willing myself to sleep, but all I could think of were defenses against imaginary attacks on Pearl and Win-win.

I forced myself to keep planning ahead. I ignored the fact that it was all on the rather shaky premise that Pearl would want to move here with me. But suddenly the thoughts took on a different quality, not of excitement, but of fear.

Win-win would need a place to go to school. What were the entrance requirements like? What paperwork was needed? And friends. I thought of how at ease Win-win was in his own village, on his scooter or just kicking a ball around in the courtyard with his neighbors. Here he would have to start over. How hard might it be for a little boy with no Cantonese to make friends in Hong Kong?

And Pearl, being Pearl, would probably want to find work in Hong Kong, but I wasn't sure if that would even be possible—legal—if she were on a one-way permit. Maybe she could do some volunteering, and take some interest classes...But would she be happy here, without work and without her mother? She was a remarkably independent and resilient person—but with the start of the school year I would be back at work from 7:30 to 5 p.m. every day, and some evenings too, for drama rehearsals, so without a job she and Win-win would be on their own quite a lot. Would they be alright?

The scariest part of the whole thing was that Pearl and I hadn't discussed any of this at all. I didn't know what she thought about building a future with me. What if all this was a summer fling to her? My heart clenched at the thought of this. *Tomorrow*, I thought. We'd talk things over tomorrow.

Finally, just as sleep felt within reach, I heard the loud buzz of my cell phone against the marble of the coffee table.

I attempted to ignore it, but I knew it was a losing battle. I was like one of Pavlov's dogs, hopelessly conditioned. What if Mom or Dad was in some kind emergency? Reluctantly, I sat up.

I unplugged my phone from the charging cable and immediately saw the first message, which was so short it fit in the preview window: *I miss you, hon*

Oh, God. It was Lindsay. In the first weeks of the summer, I had waited with my phone in my hand around the clock, desperate for a message like this. How I had wanted to get back together. At that point, I hadn't cared that she had cheated on me for over a year. I could have forgiven anything.

The phone slipped out of my sweaty, shaking hand and clattered onto the marble before promptly buzzing again. In the silence of the apartment, the noise seemed deafening. My eyes flickered towards the bedroom door. I listened carefully but didn't think the sound had woken Pearl or Win-win.

The phone had fallen face up, so I could read the next message without reaching for it: *Haven't stopped thinking about you since this afternoon x*

'Lin, stop,' I pleaded, not realizing I had said the words aloud. 'Please, don't do this.'

It buzzed again, relentless.

This time it was a photo. I was disgusted with myself for unlocking my phone to see it, but the compulsion was so strong I felt powerless against it.

It was a picture of the tattoo at the base of her spine, the one with the two intertwined L's. It was the same one I had on my lower back. We got them done together on our third anniversary; Lindsay had created the design herself. It was our secret back then: both of us being teachers, we couldn't have the tattoos somewhere more visible, but the secrecy had made the whole thing seem all the more exciting. The caption on the photo read *I want to see yours*

I felt hot with shame and guilt but when the phone buzzed again I knew better than to look at it. I jammed my thumb on the power button and held it there for far longer than the required three seconds. I threw it on the rug, hard, before burying myself under the covers. I cursed myself for not having the courage to tell her right then and there that I was in a relationship with Pearl and to stop contacting me. *She has no right to know what's going on in my life, anymore*, I told myself. *I don't have to explain anything to her.*

An hour later, I was still awake, tossing and turning on the futon. I normally didn't mind it but tonight it felt very stiff and thin, and I could feel exactly where the three folds met. There seemed to be a mosquito in the living room, too; every so often I could hear a buzzing in my ear. Or was it the phone? I felt like I needed to go and check that it was actually switched off, but I was terrified that Lindsay may have sent another message. I didn't know what I would do if she did. I touched the base of my spine a few times, willing the almost imperceptibly raised surface of the tattoo to disappear. I would have to get it removed.

I finally recognized that I was not going to be able to fall asleep anytime soon. I switched on my Chromebook and busied myself with feverishly researching the required documents for obtaining one-way permits, and potential kindergartens and primary schools for Win-win. *She hasn't said yes*, I reminded myself. *But she probably will. I think.*

A lot of what I was reading was not good news — Pearl and Win-win wouldn't be able to get one-way permits for maybe four years, and without a one-way permit, she wouldn't be able to work. I didn't have a problem with this; I had savings, and my savings and teacher's salary would be sufficient for the three of us. But I suspected Pearl wouldn't feel comfortable with this; I thought back to how confident she had been talking about her duties at the kindergarten, the joy she had in seeing Win-win each day in her role as a teacher's assistant. She'd even refused to let me pay for the souvenirs at the gift shop in Disneyland — this was very different from Lindsay, who had loved it when I paid for meals and bought her presents. It wasn't that I earned more than her. Lindsay just liked the feeling of being spoiled. Who was I kidding? I had loved treating her like royalty, too.

I rubbed my eyes and forced myself to focus on what I was reading on the computer screen. Upon marriage — *you are getting way ahead of yourself, buddy*, the voice in my head piped up — Pearl and Win-win would be entitled to extended two-way permits, which would enable them to stay in Hong Kong for three months at a time. To re-enter they would have to visit the mainland, but these trips could be short, and anyway, I was sure Pearl would want to see her mother as often as she could. The best part was that, as my stepson, Win-win would be allowed to study at any DSS or private school that would accept him. A fresh wave of worry hit me—surely the schools would see past his lack of both Cantonese and English and appreciate him for the sweet-natured, clever little boy that he was? What would we do if we couldn't find him a school?

My eyes began to droop at the 5 a.m. mark, and this time, when I collapsed on the futon, sleep did not elude me.

The next morning I was woken by a familiar and much dreaded sensation: the throbbing pain of a headache at the base of my neck. I massaged it gingerly, knowing this was just the start. When I opened my eyes, I could tell from the strength of the sun's rays that it had to be late morning already. I sat up immediately, embarrassed. What a poor host I was turning out to be!

There was a good smell in the air, a comforting, homey smell. After a moment, I recognized it for what it was—congee simmering on the stove. I spied my cell phone on the rug, and a voice in my head piped up: *What about Lindsay's messages?* I left my phone switched off and stood up, the hammering at the back of my head increasing as I did.

Pearl and Win-win were seated at the dining table, Pearl with a steaming coffee mug in her hand, and Win-win bent over a drawing. The digital clock on the piano read 10:48.

'Sorry,' I croaked. I cleared my throat, tried again. 'Sorry I woke up so late.'

Pearl put down her mug and parted her lips, about to

speak, when Win-win jumped in with his own cheery greeting: 'Morning, Leo Shushu! I'm drawing a picture of Disneyland for Ah Meh, want to see it?'

'Maybe a bit later, Win,' Pearl said gently. 'Leo Shushu probably wants to brush his teeth and have some breakfast first.'

Win-win shrugged good-naturedly and turned back to his drawing. I glanced at it anyway, gave him a thumbs-up and a wink. He grinned, continuing to add long hair to a stick person that had to be Pearl.

'I made congee,' Pearl continued shyly, heading to the stove. 'I'll heat it up for you.'

Despite my headache, I couldn't resist joining her there and wrapping my arms around her waist behind her. 'Morning, my love,' I murmured, nuzzling the back of her neck — gently, though, as I hadn't shaved in three days. A soft gasp escaped her lips; I felt her body weaken against mine. But she straightened again, wriggling out of my grasp. 'Not now,' she said into my ear, glancing at Win-win. She pecked me primly on the cheek instead. 'Go wash up while I get your congee ready.'

I quickly brushed my teeth and give my face a rigorous rub with the washcloth. The cold water seemed to help a little.

When I returned to the living room, I saw that my futon and bedding had been put away. On the table was a steaming bowl of congee and a cup of tea on one of my grey placemats. 'It's only plain,' Pearl said, handing me a ceramic soup spoon. 'I found the rice tub under the sink.'

Maybe it was because I didn't feel well, but the congee brought to mind a flood of childhood memories. Mom only ever made congee for me when I was sick. Children don't usually like bland rice porridge, they associate it with illness and the elderly, but the taste always made me feel loved, finally worthy of my mother's attention. She always took the day off work when we were sick. When Henry and I were in good health, which was most of the time, our helpers did the cooking, cleaning, and childminding. Our parents, one a lawyer and the other a teacher turned school principal, were always very busy. They had mellowed out tremendously since they retired a few years ago — Mom actually enjoyed cooking now, and Dad was obsessed with his bread maker.

Pearl's congee was different from Mom's. While Mom's was always perfectly smooth, Pearl's was chunkier, heartier; she had allowed some of the grains of rice to retain their shape and chewy texture. Mom normally flavored her congee with liberal amounts of salted egg chunks and pulled pork, my favorite toppings, but Pearl's was, of course, plain. I had no fresh ingredients in the flat. Yet she had somehow managed to work magic into the congee — it was richer and more flavorful than boiled rice had any right in being. I couldn't think of anything I'd rather eat than this warm bowl of congee that Pearl had cooked for me.

'Is it okay?' Pearl asked anxiously.

I swallowed my mouthful of congee, realizing I hadn't said anything. 'Oh, Pearl, it's so good. I don't think I've ever had anything so good.'

She reddened at my praise. 'I can make it for you whenever you want.' She looked down at her hands. 'I am happy you like it.'

'My mama can make anything,' Win-win added helpfully. He was now making little lines, presumably grass, along the bottom edge of the paper. I was impressed by how careful he was about stopping every time he reached the edge so he didn't make draw marks on the table.

'Thank you so much,' I said. I wanted to say more, but my headache was worsening — the tension had spread from my neck upwards to the back of my head, but also downwards, to my shoulders and upper back. I closed my eyes for a moment, trying to get a handle on the pain. 'I'm sorry I woke up so late. I... didn't sleep well last night.' I needed to get some Panadol in my system, and fast.

Pearl watched me intently as I spoke and I had the distinct sensation that she could see through me. Without saying anything, she got up behind me and placed her hands on the sides of my head. 'You're hurting,' she murmured. I nodded reluctantly, helplessly. 'Let me help.'

She began kneading the back of my neck, my shoulders, and her touch was surprisingly firm and intuitive; she seemed to know exactly where I was hurting most, though if she had asked me I would have struggled to pinpoint them. Part of me wanted to squirm out of her reach, the pain was so intense. When she began applying pressure to the base of my skull, where the pain was worst, it was all I could do not to cry out.

And yet it was not long before I felt relief; the knots in my back and shoulders, behind my eyes, in my neck — I could almost see them loosening and relinquishing their grip on me. When only a ghost of the headache remained, I placed my hands over Pearl's, stopping her. 'Whoa,' I managed. 'You saved me.'

She blushed again. She didn't say anything, just kissed me on my right temple before sitting down again.

'Done,' Win-win announced, holding up his drawing. It was quite good — the castle was immediately recognizable, with turrets and battlements, and he had even added some energetic red and orange streaks — fireworks — to the sky. Pearl wrapped her hand around Win-win's and helped him to write his name and the date on the bottom right corner. I found a roll of masking tape in one of the kitchen drawers and stuck the drawing up on the shoe cabinet.

'That might be your best one yet,' I declared, ruffling his hair.

He turned bright red. He was like his mom in that way; it was as if neither of them was accustomed to hearing praise.

Pearl said something softly to him in Min, to which he nodded eagerly. She took out her phone and tapped at it a few times until it was playing a cartoon in Putonghua. He settled down with it on the sofa.

'Are you really better?' Pearl asked, her brow furrowed. 'You looked so pale just now.'

'I wasn't feeling so good earlier,' I admitted, 'but I'm a lot better now. I didn't sleep very well last night.'

'You should rest some more,' she said, tucking a lock of hair behind her ear in a gesture that was lovely and demure. 'I was thinking of taking Win-win out for a walk anyway. I want to buy a few things at the grocery store.'

'Sure. I'll come with you. I'm not tired.' But before I could say any more, I found myself yawning. 'Excuse me.'

Pearl grinned. 'Please. Rest a little more. We can go out in the afternoon, if you want, whatever you like. But you need to rest first.'

I stifled another yawn. 'Let me draw you a map, at least,' I insisted, grabbing a sheet of paper from the printer and sketching a quick map for her, just in case. I so wanted to take care of them, but I was doing a lousy job. 'It's only a ten-minute walk, but you should take an umbrella. There's no shade along the way.'

She studied the drawing, tracing the path from this building to the store with her index finger. 'Actually, the reason I wanted to go the grocery store is because I'd like to cook lunch for you later. Fujian-style. Is that okay?'

When I licked my lips, she blushed with pleasure. I grabbed two of my cloth shopping bags for Pearl, then handed her the spare keys, my Octopus card, and the umbrella with the black UV lining. 'If it isn't too sunny, maybe Win can play for a bit in the playground.'

Win-win stood up immediately. 'I'll go pee first!'

Pearl quickly cleared the table before disappearing into my bedroom to change. When she returned, she was wearing a summery floral sundress, and her hair was tied up in a pretty French braid that ran down her back. 'I think I want to go with you guys after all,' I said, not wanting to be apart.

'Absolutely not. Go back to bed inside,' Pearl ordered, for the third time, then softened her tone: 'I love you.' She stood on her tiptoes and pecked me on the lips. Win-win gave me a high-five before they headed out to wait for the elevator.

'Come back soon!' I called. I knew they were still there, waiting, even though I could no longer see them around the corner. Win-win responded with a cheery 'We will!' just as the doors of the elevator slammed shut.

The apartment was suddenly so quiet. It felt odd and unfamiliar, even though this was how it always used to be. Already that life on my own seemed to be something from the distant past, a memory. I took two Panadol tablets with a swig of water before heading into my bedroom.

I climbed into my bed and pulled the covers up to my chin, pleasantly surprised by how different it smelled after just two days. It smelled of Pearl — it had to be whatever products she used on her face, her body — and it smelled sweet and clean and right.

I fell asleep thinking of Pearl, but my dreams were troubled. We were at Disneyland, or someplace like it. Pearl was wearing the cream blouse with the lace collar and purple skirt from yesterday, but she was facing away from me. When she spoke, though, I heard Lindsay's American accent. She turned slowly around and I realized with cold certainty that it *was* Lindsay, before she cut her hair so short. Lindsay pulled the waist band of Pearl's skirt down, just an inch or so, enough to show me the double L tattoo at the base of her spine. Suddenly, she was next to me. 'I want to see yours too,' she whispered sultrily into my ear. 'Where's yours, Leo? Where's yours?'

I was woken by the sound of the doorbell followed by someone knocking loudly on the door. Deeply relieved to find that I was safely in my bed, without Lindsay, and that the knocking and ringing were coming from the front door, I scrambled out of bed, rushing to the living room. As I was opening the door, prepared to apologize to Pearl and Win-win for making them wait so long, I remembered that I had given them the spare keys; they wouldn't have rung the doorbell.

Standing at the doorstep was my mother, weighed down with several shopping bags bulging with fruit and thermos bottles. She looked flustered, almost embarrassed. She began talking at once, her face red: 'Morning, I know you don't like it when I just show up like this, you've told me many times and of course I understand, but I've been calling you all morning and you didn't pick up, so —'

My phone! I hadn't touched it since last night, after Lindsay texted. 'Sorry, Mom; it's not your fault — I didn't remember to turn my phone on. Let me help you with your things —'

She laid out her gifts neatly on the dining table: clementines, a large Glad-wrapped wedge of watermelon, green *and* purple grapes, bread rolls, no doubt fresh from Dad's bread maker, and two thermoses. There was hardly any room left on my little square dining table, she'd brought so much food.

'I made soup for you this morning, it's your favorite — green radish and carrot,' she said, unscrewing the cap from one of the thermoses. She gestured at the other. 'And that's congee for lunch. I added an extra salted egg for you. I know you like the yolk.'

'Thanks, Mom,' I said. I fixed her a cup of tea and we sat down at the dining table together. 'You brought me so many nice things.' Glancing at the clock, I could see it would have been over an hour and a half since Pearl and Win-win left for their grocery run, and they would be home any moment now. I tried not to look as panicked as I felt. How long was Mom planning on staying?

'Well, I worried that you might not have much in your fridge, after just coming home —' She headed to the drying rack beside the sink, wanting to get me a bowl for the soup, but paused at the half-finished pot of congee Pearl had left to cool on the stove.

'But you don't know how to cook congee.' She said this as though she was responding to a question that no one asked. Her eyes were suddenly opened to the changes in my apartment: the giant Simba toy, with Wuwu perched on his head, the crayon drawings that we had masking-taped to the shoe cabinet, Pearl's pink neck fan, Win-win's green sandals.

'Do you have company?' she finally asked, hesitantly. She poured out a bowl of soup and pushed it towards me. 'It isn't Lindsay, is it?' She was trying so hard not to sound hopeful.

'Mom, I'm sorry — it's over between me and Lindsay.'

She was deeply disappointed, that much was clear, but she put on a brave face. 'Never mind, dear, it won't be long until you find someone like her, I'm sure —'

I didn't know how to respond to this, but for Pearl's sake I felt I had to try. 'Actually, Mom, I've been meaning to —'

But just then, I heard the muted *ding!* of the elevator reaching the top floor, mine. This was followed by the sound of footsteps — one quicker pair running, the other walking more slowly, unmistakably making their way towards my door. I could hear

JANE LO

Pearl calling out a reminder, a warning, and Win-win's footsteps slowed down immediately.

Together, we listened to the jangle of keys, then a key being inserted into the lock.

Chapter 19
Pearl

'Hi,' Leo said, opening the door for us and relieving me of my cloth carrying bag. His tone seemed tighter than I remembered, his smile strained. Had we been gone for too long? We *had* taken a bit longer than I expected; Win-win enjoyed the playground so much, had played on the swings for ages, and I'd had such fun perusing the aisles at the supermarket, which didn't look very big from the outside but was actually a treasure trove of goodies. The prices were a bit higher than back home, but not outrageously so, so I let Win-win choose a few packs of chips and biscuits. They had the craziest potato chip flavors, everything from roast goose flavor to scrambled eggs with tomato flavor. In the end, we decided we couldn't pass up on the chance to try the Hong Kong-style sweet and sour pork flavored chips, given how much we loved the actual dish.

They even had the right kind of baby oyster for the omelettes I was planning to fry up for lunch, and the chives and shallots, too. I bought enough ingredients to prepare a proper feast: oyster omelettes, meatball soup, cauliflower and sliced pork, and if I had time, taro mud for dessert. The only thing the supermarket didn't have was gingko nuts, but that was okay; peanuts would do for the taro mud topping. As Win-win and I explored the aisles of the supermarket, our shopping cart slowly filling up, I had allowed myself to just live in the present, not thinking beyond today. I was on a mission to prepare the heartiest, tastiest lunch for the people I loved.

But now, with Leo looking inexplicably solemn, I felt a weight in my gut, like I had eaten a bowl of undercooked noodles that I couldn't digest. The air felt so tense I could almost feel its weight on my shoulders as the three of us crowded around the door. Win-win, oblivious to all this, kicked off his sandals and pushed past us. Leo leaned close to me, as though he was about to kiss me. He spoke so softly I could barely hear him: 'My mom's here. She just showed up. Sorry.'

With great effort I nodded and smiled.

The table was covered from edge to edge with food, and suddenly I felt foolish for thinking that Leo might need me to cook for him. His mother was sitting at the table, her eyes darting between me and Win-win, her expression one of pure bewilderment. She was an attractive woman: in her sixties, perhaps, stylishly dressed in a striped silk blouse with a large heart-shaped jade pendant upon her neck. Her wavy chin-length hair was dyed a youthful auburn color; there wasn't a grey hair in sight. It must take a lot of time and money to maintain that sort of hairstyle. I felt a sudden wave of longing for my own mother.

'Hello, Auntie,' Win-win said, solemnly. He was standing with his hands pressed to his sides, the way he did at assembly when the kindergarten principal was about to address the school.

'Hello, Auntie,' I repeated, bowing my head. I suddenly remembered something—hurrying into Leo's room, I grabbed the can of tea I brought for his parents, in case an encounter like this should happen. Ma had insisted.

'Auntie, this is for you. It is from my hometown.' I handed it to her with both hands and she took it, murmuring her thanks.

She finally smiled at us, but the smile didn't quite reach her eyes—they appraised me and Win-win in a way that made it clear she had already decided she didn't like us. 'Hello,' she finally said, tentatively. 'It's nice to meet you.'

Leo, who had been stuffing the contents of the bag into the refrigerator, rushed over to join us at the table. He cleared his throat. 'Mom, this is Pearl, and this is her little boy, Win-win. They're visiting from Xiamen.' He placed one hand on the small of my back and the other on Win's shoulder. 'Pearl, Win-win, this is my mom.'

Everyone awkwardly repeated their hellos. She continued regarding us with undisguised suspicion. Win-win quietly escaped to the rug and began stacking dominos into tottery structures. I wished I could join him.

'So, you met this summer?' Although she said this in very poor Putonghua, she managed to make it sound like an accusation. I wanted to tell her that I could understand Cantonese, but also didn't want her to feel like I was criticizing her.

'Yes, about a month ago.' I made sure my body language was open, the way I was when I was when speaking with a tourist who hadn't decided if she trusted me. The living room, with its high ceilings and large windows, was normally so airy and spacious, but today it felt cramped and hot. My armpits were growing damp and although I did roll on a bit of deodorant this morning, I desperately hoped the dreaded dark patches weren't beginning to appear on my dress. 'Leo was visiting Xiamen at the time, and I...I showed him around.'

'Did you, now? How lovely.' For a moment I wondered if I should explain that he had paid me to do so. When had we crossed over to the other side—from service provider and client to friends, to lovers? I could see the gears turning in Leo's mother's head: surely it was not every day that people invited their tour guide home to stay?

I realized that Leo had picked up where I left off. '...was amazing, Mom, she took me to all the best places. Pearl's also a great cook, her mom too—'

Her mom's eyes narrowed slightly, as though she were trying not to feel jealous. This I could understand—Ma could get that way even when I was complimenting Third Aunt on her cooking.

Leo continued, oblivious: '...and she's got her own fields, grows her own vegetables... carrots, cauliflower, shallots, even peanuts...and they've got a little orchard, haven't you, Pearl, with two longan trees and a mango tree—'

I liked listening to Leo remember our village so fondly, but his mother nodded impatiently, clearly uninterested. 'And how do you like Hong Kong so far? You like it here?'

I wanted to like Leo's mom—but her questions made me feel nervous. Should I say it was nicer than Xiamen? Was that the answer she expected?

'I like it,' I finally said, trying hard to smile naturally. 'It's our first time here, and Leo's taken such good care of us. We went to Disneyland yesterday, and it was—'

'Oh yes,' she interrupted. A shadow crossed her face. 'My daughter-in-law mentioned seeing you there.'

Maybe I was being paranoid but her tone suggested that Melissa had caught Leo and I doing something shameful.

She took a sip from her cup before regarding me again. 'And how much longer will you be staying here?'

'Just a few more days,' I murmured, my cheeks burning. Why did everything she say sound accusatory?

'Right,' Leo interjected, a bit too loudly. 'Mom, Pearl and I, we're—'

Her phone rang then, and she held up her hand as Leo opened his mouth to speak. I noticed that her nails were painted a beautiful rose gold color, really elegant. 'Just a minute, Leo; it's your father.'

We'd been standing all this time in front of the table, as though we were students being interrogated by a teacher. Leo pulled out a chair for me and we both sat down.

'Hi, love,' she said. To my surprise her voice took on a sweet, almost girlish quality as she spoke with her husband, and despite all my misgivings about her I was touched. What would it be like to still be so in love at sixty? I had never seen a marriage like that before. Ba left Ma before they even made it two years, and Hong and were never married at all. Back in the village, couples were rarely so open about their love; affection was expressed through good cooking, through bringing home the month's paycheck. Romantic words were rarely spoken, at least not in public. I glanced at Leo and realized he had been looking at me too. Was he thinking about a future together, as I was? But would his parents ever approve of such a match? And if they didn't— would he fight for me? Was I worth fighting for?

'I'm still at Leo's. Mm-hmm. Yes. Just a few more minutes. I'll be back in time for a late lunch. Mm, yes, that's right. I'll ask him, tell him to call you back. Bye.' She slipped her phone back into her handbag. 'Daddy wants to know if you're coming to Maa Maa's birthday party on Sunday.' She hesitated. 'You *did* remember, didn't you? That's why you came back this week?'

I suspected that Leo had forgotten; he hadn't said anything about this birthday celebration at all. For a split-second he seemed to be at a loss for words, but he quickly recovered: 'Of course, Mom. It's Maa Maa's 90th; I'd never miss that.'

She nodded approvingly as she stood up. 'Good. You *are* her favorite. She's always telling everyone that.' She glanced at me, then shielded her mouth with the back of her hand as she whispered something conspiratorially in English to Leo. I caught Lindsay's name, but I couldn't understand the rest as it was spoken so quickly.

He reddened, and for the first time since his mother arrived, I saw a flash of anger cross his face. 'Mom, I've told you over and over—there's no chance of that.' He said this in Cantonese, for my benefit. 'Please stop.'

She shrugged, nonplussed. She continued in Cantonese: 'Fine. Just thought it'd be a nice surprise for your grandma. You know how fond Grandma is of her.' She slung her leather handbag over one shoulder. 'Wait—you were saying something when Daddy called.' She sat back down, expectant. 'What was it?'

I didn't need Leo to make a grand announcement about me right now. It was obvious that this would be terrible timing. But as I tried to shake my head in his direction without being too obvious about it, Leo nodded. 'Mom, I know this will come as a surprise…and I wasn't trying to keep it a secret from you when I was on the mainland. I just wanted to tell you in person that Pearl is more than just a friend.' He continued, as though he couldn't see that his mother looked completely shell-shocked and not at all pleased. 'We're in love. I love Pearl so much, Mom, I—'

'*What* did you say?' She said this so sharply, so loudly, that Win-win's head snapped towards us, fear in his eyes. I balled my hands into fists to stop them from trembling. 'You *just* met her,' she cried, her displeasure no longer veiled. 'You're joking, aren't you, this is your idea of a good joke—'

On the surface, Leo didn't seem particularly alarmed by his mother's outburst, but I could see beads of sweat popping on his forehead. 'It *has* been a bit of a whirlwind,' he said. 'But you're always telling me how Dad fell in love with you *at first sight*.' I felt a great surge of love for him. 'Isn't that right, Mom?'

'I knew this was going to happen,' she continued bitterly, ignoring him. 'You're so *pure*, so *good*, you never see the bad in *anyone*...I should've stopped you from running off to the mainland, you were so vulnerable, after what happened with Lindsay...I just knew you were going to be tricked, cheated out of your house and home by a—'

I strove to keep my expression impassive, although it hurt to be spoken about like this, right in front of me. *Maybe she doesn't know I understand what she's saying. She's only trying to protect her son. You'd be worried, wouldn't you, if Win-win...*

'Nobody tricked me,' Leo interrupted calmly, his tone matter-of-fact. 'It's not like that at all. I'm turning forty in a few weeks, Mom. I feel so lucky to have met Pearl. Once you get to know her, Mom, you'll see that—'

'This is so outrageous I can't even talk to you right now. I'm going home. I'm going to tell your father exactly what is going on here, and let him be the one to—'

'Mom, don't be like this,' he pleaded. 'I...I love her.' I felt tears prickling my eyes. 'That's what really matters, isn't it?'

His mother frowned. She took one last angry look at me before grabbing her handbag and jamming her feet in her shoes. The bang of the front door reverberated through the flat.

Chapter 20
Leo

We had more than enough food for lunch — two kinds of congee, bread rolls, soup, watermelon for dessert — but Pearl was already at the fridge, frantically pulling out ingredients — eggs, a tub of something that could be oysters, a head of cauliflower.

She cracked six eggs into the mixing bowl with much more force than necessary and beat them mercilessly with a pair of chopsticks, the only sound in the apartment the incessant *ping ping ping* of melamine plastic against glass. I wanted to go to her, hold her, reassure her that while things with Mom could be like this, she always came around — almost always, anyway — but Pearl's expression was so angry I didn't dare interrupt her.

Instead, I sat down with Win-win on the rug, where he had created a little domino city and was gently pushing two battered Hot Wheels around the buildings. 'Can I play, too?'

'Sure,' he said eagerly, pressing one of the cars into my palm. 'Leo Shushu, you drive this one.' He demonstrated how to navigate the car on the rug between the buildings while vrooming under his breath. Playing with Win-win was so quiet and easy; unlike with Corrie, who insisted on holding long, involved conversations about everything from Disney princesses to endangered species to dwarf planets, Win-win was content to have both of us vrooming quietly around the little white and black structures.

I joined Pearl in the kitchen area, leaning casually against the fridge. 'Hey,' I said quietly. 'You doing okay?'

She slid the glistening oyster pancake onto a ceramic plate without answering. The pancake was slightly too big for the plate; my stomach growled at the sight of it.

'I think we need to talk,' she finally said.

'Okay.'

She wiped the counter with a paper towel, avoiding eye contact with me. 'I mean…your mother's right, we just met. Maybe—'

'I think maybe she was just surprised.' But this didn't come out right; it sounded callous and unfeeling, so I followed it up with: 'How can she not like you?', but the intonation was off, and it sounded like an actual question rather than a rhetorical one.

She silently arranged the bowls and chopsticks around the dishes of food: a glistening cauliflower stir-fry, the oyster pancake, a large steaming bowl of noodles and tiny meatballs. 'Wash your hands, Win,' she said quietly. The little boy immediately abandoned his dominos and sprinted to the washroom.

Once Win-win was out of earshot, she continued: 'I…I didn't know your mom was bringing food,' she said, shaking her head. 'I wanted to cook for you, to say thank you—'

Win-win returned from the washroom and looked curiously at his mother, who had buried her head in her hands. 'Mama?'

'I'm fine,' she managed, but her voice cracked. The heels of her hands swiped desperately at her eyes.

Win-win promptly climbed onto her lap and blotted her cheeks with a tissue with a practiced hand. He gave me a look, one that said *She does this sometimes, just give her a moment* — and I marveled that this child, not yet five, could understand his mother like this. Satisfied that his mother was going to be alright, he slid back onto the floor and went to his seat. He looked longingly at the food at the table, but sat with his hands folded, waiting for the adults' okay.

My own stomach growling, I filled the three bowls with noodles. Pearl finally looked up, her eyes swollen. She murmured, 'Let's eat.' Her hands trembling, she reached for the ladle in my hand. This time, she didn't bristle at my touch. Together, we topped up the bowls with more soup and meatballs. 'Eat while it's hot.'

I knew my judgment was clouded by how hungry I was, but the food was *so* good. The tiny meatballs were filled with a surprise, a rich, meaty broth, and the silky noodles were so smooth and fine they kept slipping off my chopsticks. I resorted to shoveling them into my mouth with a soup spoon, the way Win-win was doing. Pearl had even prepared a dipping sauce, something tart and sweet with just a hint of heat that went with everything, but matched the crispy oyster pancake best. When I said, 'Pearl, I've never had anything so delicious,' her cheeks reddened immediately, a smile tugging at her lips, but I meant it. 'Thank you.' I reached for her hand, and was relieved when she didn't pull away. I lowered my voice: 'I'll talk to my parents. Don't worry.' I ladled another generous helping of noodles into my bowl, and Win-win's.

'My turn,' I announced at the end of the meal, when everyone, even Win-win, was sipping tea. 'Why don't you and Win-win watch a little TV while I wash up?'

Pearl shook her head. 'Let me do it, you go sit—'

But I insisted, herding them towards the sofa with my outstretched arms, as though they were sheep, despite their protests. I fiddled with the laptop, projecting the Netflix home page on the television. Win-win squealed with pleasure and rushed to the TV screen. He pointed at the Paw Patrol icon, then changed his mind and chose Animal Mechanicals. 'Louder, please, Mama,' Win-win said, his eyes fixed on the screen.

Content that they were comfortable, I turned back to the sink. Pearl had washed the pot and frying pan already, and wiped down the counters, so there wasn't much left—just our dishes, bowls and chopsticks. As the sink filled with warm water, I put on my Bluetooth headset and called Dad.

He picked up on the second ring. 'Hi, Dad.' I squeezed some detergent onto a sponge and began washing the bowls, careful to make as little noise as possible. I glanced at Pearl and Win-win, who didn't seem to have noticed that I was on the phone.

'It's Leo,' I heard him murmuring, presumably to Mom, before he addressed me. 'How nice of you to finally tell your parents about your new girlfriend! Your mother is very upset, and so am I. How secretive of you! Unacceptable!'

Dad's tone didn't match his words; it was obvious that Mom had asked him to reprimand me, and given him the words to say, too. All his life Mom had tried to force him into the mold of a stern father, but Dad had always been gentler, milder, than Mom. Even when we were kids, when he was telling us off, it always felt like he was playing a part, and not very well. I wondered if he was privately happy for me, but not allowed to show it.

'I was going to call you this morning, Dad, but then Mom came over. I wasn't trying to hide anything. Honestly.'

This was mostly true. I could have mentioned something to them when I was still in Xiamen, but it would have been even worse; they would certainly have tried to convince me to break things off.

'Well,' Dad said, clearly struggling to stay upset, 'well, it would have been better, more sensible, you know, if you'd taken your time to get to know her before inviting her into your home, and we would of course have appreciated being kept in the loop... But, you know,' he said, a note of wonder in his voice, 'you haven't sounded so happy in months.' I heard the scratchy sound of his thumb covering the mic, then, a muffled 'Well, honey, it's true, isn't it?'

I felt a weight lifting from my shoulders. With Dad on my side, Mom would come around eventually, surely.

Dad coughed. 'Your mom says Pearl is a mother already...?' I could hear the doubt creeping back into his voice. 'She has a little boy?'

I began rinsing the cutlery under a weak stream of cold water. 'Yes, Win-win's nearly five. He's the sweetest little boy I've ever met. You're going to love him, Dad. I promise.'

He made a non-committal sound. 'And she's from...?'

'Xiamen. She was my tour guide.'

'She's a tour guide?' Dad echoed weakly.

I switched off the tap and dried my hands on a paper towel, trying not to be offended. Mom and Dad would never admit to being snobs, but they did quietly look down on anyone who wasn't a *professional*. They would far prefer that their daughter-in-law was a nice professional girl, not a working-class woman.

'She works at a kindergarten during the school year, but in the summers, she takes tourists on day trips and things.'

'So, a teacher like you, then,' he said, clearly relieved.

I sat down at the table and took a sip of tea, now cold. Mouse was transforming into her mechanical self, her legs extending into the front wheels of a racecar. 'Mechana, can we do it? *We Animal Mechanical can!*' Win-win's eyes were glued to the screen, but Pearl was swiping on her phone, her expression pensive. She was right—we needed to talk. 'I gotta go, Dad. Nice talking to you. See you at Grandma's party.'

'You're...not going to bring...?'

I hadn't really thought about whether I should bring Pearl or Win-win, honestly. It would be stressful for Pearl to face my tactless and overbearing extended family, but also odd to not bring her, now that I'd told Mom and Dad about her. 'You don't want me to?'

'Honestly, it does seem a bit soon, but I'm sure your grandmother will be pleased to meet her.' He hesitated. 'I guess it's up to you.'

'I'll talk to Pearl, then.'

We said our goodbyes. I went to join Pearl and Win-win in front of the TV.

Sitting cross-legged on the rug, I leaned against Pearl's legs. A moment later, I felt her hands on my shoulders, kneading them.

I reached for them, wrapping her arms around my neck like a scarf. This made her giggle. 'I love you,' she suddenly said, tenderly. 'I'm sorry for all the trouble I'm causing. I'm happy here with you. So very happy. Honest.'

I reached for her hand and kissed the little web of skin between her thumb and her index finger. I heard the faintest gasp behind me. 'Want to talk inside for a moment?'

'Yes, please,' she murmured. Then, clearing her throat, she said, 'Win-win, ten more minutes, okay? Leo Shushu and I need talk for a while.'

His eyes still on the TV screen, he smiled and nodded. 'Sure, Mama.'

———〜〜〜———

When we reached the bedroom, I closed the door softly behind me. Win-win would be fine for just a few minutes; I could hear the Animal Mechanicals theme song; it was the start of another episode. Pearl, who perched on the edge of the bed, made no objection. 'Kiss me,' she whispered.

And when I did, I found Pearl's touch—her lips, her hands—as needy and urgent as mine. 'I love you,' she finally said, slightly out of breath.

I grinned. 'I know.'

But her expression was serious. 'I'm also scared.'

Me too. 'My mom, right?'

She shook her head. 'Not just her.' She hesitated. 'People don't really talk like this back home. But I feel like you're the one for me.' She looked away, suddenly shy. 'Do you feel that way about me?'

I smiled broadly, touched by her words. 'You know how I told you I couldn't sleep last night?'

She rested her head on my shoulder. 'Yes.'

'I did some research.'

Slipping her hand in mine, she waited for me to continue.

'I was thinking that if maybe you decided you wanted to—' Now it was my turn to blush. 'Like, if we wanted to continue being…together…one option could be that maybe you and Win could come to live with me in Hong Kong.'

Pearl sat up immediately, her eyes wide. 'Do you mean that?'

'I do,' I said, softly. 'I mean it with all my heart. But only if you want to. It would be a big change for you and Win, to leave Xiamen, and your mom. So, no pressure—'

'But what about *your* mom? She was upset that we were here at all. If she found out that you were thinking of…you know—' She frowned. 'She's going to be furious.'

'Maybe so,' I agreed, 'but maybe not for long. She'll come around. And even if she doesn't at first—' I lifted my shoulders in a half-shrug. 'I won't let that affect us.'

'Leo…do you mean getting married?'

I gazed at her face, trying to determine the response she was looking for. 'I don't think we have to decide right now, but I love you very, very much. If later on...after you've lived here for a bit...and you decide that you like it, and you like...me —' I let my voice trail off. 'I would love for us to get married.'

She rested her head on my shoulder and slipped her arm through mine. 'I can't believe this isn't a dream. I kept worrying that maybe after this week...you would want to return to your real life in Hong Kong. The one you had before you met me and Win.'

'You *are* my real life now.' I kissed her forehead. 'And you know what they say in *Titanic*.'

Pearl grinned, sitting up again. 'What?'

I reached into to the drawer on my desk. I hadn't planned this moment, but it was as good a time as any. 'Close your eyes and hold out your hand.' She did, obediently. I took the pendant and necklace out of its velvet box and placed it on her palm. 'This is for you.'

She laughed when she saw the cactus. 'I love it! I love it so much!'

'See what it says on the back first.'

She turned it over, then squinted at the tiny letters on the back. '*You jump, I jump,*' she read in a careful staccato. She giggled even as her eyes filled with tears. 'Oh, Leo!'

At her request, I helped her put it on. Just as I was closing the clasp, I heard Win-win knocking on the door. 'Mama,' he said, 'can I start a new episode or do I have to stop now?'

Pearl regained her composure immediately. 'I'm coming,' she said, wiping her eyes with the back of her hand as she stood up. 'You should probably stop.'

'Pearl,' I said quietly. 'Can you help me with something?'

'Of course,' she said. 'What is it?'

'I need some help choosing something...do you and Win-win mind going out to do some shopping with me?'

'Of course not. We'd love to help.'

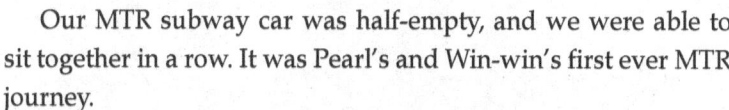

Our MTR subway car was half-empty, and we were able to sit together in a row. It was Pearl's and Win-win's first ever MTR journey.

'So, where are we going?' Pearl asked. She'd been taking lots of pictures and sending them home to her mom. She'd gotten a few in return—one of baby Xiaobei, one of the brown and white eggs the hens laid this morning—and was excited to share them with me. She'd been sending text messages, and from the smile on her face as she typed them, she was telling her mom about our conversation earlier.

I'd received my fair share of text messages, too, mostly from my deeply concerned older brother. Henry tried to call, but after I texted him and told him I was busy, he switched to irritating text messages, a barrage of them: *What's going on??? Mom said you're dating a mainlander. You're kidding, right?? Don't do anything rash. Drinks tonight? Come on, let's talk things out. Call me (asap). Are you sure this isn't a rebound relationship? Cuz that isn't fair for anybody, least of all the mainland woman you're seeing.*

This last message ws harder to ignore than the others, but I managed. I'm pretty sure Melissa fed Henry the words to that last text, and maybe all of them, so I wasn't going to hold it against him.

Win-win tugged on my shirtsleeve. 'Yeah, Leo Shushu, where? Not...not Disneyland again?' He carefully studied the MTR system map on the wall of the car with its flashing red lights, his eyes hopeful. 'But we passed Sunny Bay Station ages ago—'

A SUMMER LIKE THAT

I laughed, slipping my phone back into my jeans pocket. 'Not Disneyland today, Win. But you'll like it, I promise.'

Chapter 21
Pearl

Prince Edward MTR Exit C1 spilled us onto a crowded sidewalk, the afternoon sun hot and unforgiving. Leo led us to a small roadside park a few meters from the station where we sat down and pulled out our sun gear: Win-win donned his baseball cap, and Leo reached over to switch on my neck fan for me. With his other hand, he put on his aviator sunglasses.

I smile. 'You look like a movie star.'

'So do you,' he replied immediately, tucking a sweaty lock of hair behind my ear. 'Prettier than a movie star.' He pointed at the bubble tea shop the next block over. 'Would you like a cold drink, Win-win? Chocolate or strawberry?'

Win-win stuck out the tip of his tongue and licked his lips as though he was trying the flavors in his mind. 'Strawberry, please.'

Leo turned to me. 'Want a bubble tea?'

'No, thanks. I'll just have a bit of Win's.'

Win-win and I waited on the bench as Leo went to get the drinks. 'I picked strawberry cause it's your favorite.' He leaned against my arm, tilting his head towards me so I could see the pleased expression on his face.

He laughed as I tickled the bottom of his chin. Together we watched as Leo tapped his Octopus card on the reader, then stood to one side to wait for his order. He took out his phone and started tapping on it. 'Do you like it here, Win?'

'Yes. *Super* yes.' He swung his feet with gusto as he watched a stray cat pawing at an empty potato chip packet. 'But when are we going back home?'

My phone buzzed in my pocket. It was a selfie of Leo with puppy dog eyes. He was holding out a Korean-style finger heart, his index finger crossing his thumb. *Miss you already*, his text said.

Win-win and I sent him a selfie right back, Win-win making a big heart with both arms, the tips of his fingers touching the top of his head, and I holding up a finger heart that matched Leo's. When we looked up, giggling, we saw Leo waving at us from outside the bubble tea shop, a smile on his face.

'You were asking when we'll be going home,' I said slowly, pulling Win-win onto my lap. He was getting so heavy, more than forty pounds the last time he stood on the scale, but that was at the kindergarten, before the summer holidays. He had to be even heavier now. When I held him close, though, I found he still had his sweet little boy smell, the one I often wished I could bottle up and remember for always. I nuzzled the top of his head with my nose, the way I'd done since he was a newborn with nothing but peach fuzz for hair. 'Well, you and I are going to take the train back to Ah Meh's soon, maybe on Sunday, maybe tomorrow. But—' Here I glanced at him, trying to gauge how he really felt about all these sudden changes, but he leaned against me calmly, watching as the stray cat jumped nimbly onto the railing and strutted upon it like a tightrope artist. Was it right of me to put him through all this? What if things didn't work out? There were so many ways that things could not work out.

'Would you want to live here, someday? With Leo Shushu?'

'It might be fun,' he said agreeably. 'I like the playground.'

'But I mean for always,' I continued anxiously. 'You would go to a new school here... and I would work here, as soon as I find a job, I mean...and we would only see Ah Meh during the holidays.' I hesitated, nervous. 'What do you think, Win?'

Win-win smiled at me, that dimpled smile that I loved so much, and in that moment he looked much older and wiser than a child who was four and a half going on five. I had that uncanny feeling that he was reading my mind, and that he knew how desperately I needed him to agree to all this. It was a connection we've always had, but which I had always been afraid of taking advantage of. 'I think it's good.'

'What's good?'

I was speaking so intently to Win-win that I didn't realize that Leo had returned. He was standing in front of us, looking sheepish and clutching a cardboard tray containing three tall creamy drinks. He handed Win-win a marbled pink and white one, kept the brown milk tea with tapioca pearls for himself, and for me, he held out a pale purple drink with a matching paper straw. 'It's taro,' he said, shyly. 'I know you didn't want your own drink but it's a new flavor, and it made me think of you. If you'd rather not—'

I grabbed it from his hands and sucked hard on the straw before he could finish his sentence. It was so much like Ma's taro mud, thick and smooth and just gently sweet, with that distinctive earthiness that made taro so versatile. 'Oh, Leo,' I sighed, 'it's divine.'

The delight in his eyes was unmistakable. 'I was hoping you'd like it.' He sat down beside Win-win, who pointed out the cat to him.

Setting the drink on the bench, I called Ma, who picked up on the second ring. The image that filled my screen was incredibly vibrant: Ma had tied her hair up in a bright orange and purple scarf, and the sky was a blinding, cloudless blue behind her. Her face broke into a broad smile when she saw us. 'You called at *just* the right time! Look how big the cauliflowers have gotten! Just *look* at them, Win-win! You see Ah Meh's cauliflower?'

She switched to the back-facing camera and Win-win and Leo crowded around me as the white and green florets filled the screen.

'I was just about to harvest them,' Ma continued as we oohed and aahed appreciatively at the enormous cauliflower — it had to be nearly a foot in diameter. 'We'll have to give your parents one, Leo!'

Leo grinned. 'Thank you, Auntie. I'm sure they would love one.'

'Ah Meh,' Win-win suddenly cried. 'I miss you!'

Ma smiled fondly at Win-win. It had only been a few days, but this was the longest they'd ever been apart. I wondered again whether it was right for me to wrench Win-win from his life back home. 'Not as much as Ah Meh misses *you*! When are you coming back?'

I scooped him onto my lap as Ma continued talking. It filled my heart with joy to see my mother so happy. 'We'll be back — ' here I glanced at Leo, who gave me a smile and two thumbs up, which I took to mean *Go when you need to*, 'in the next few days, okay, Ma? I'll give you the exact time and date once I get the tickets. I'll message you.'

We said our goodbyes. Our drinks in hand, Leo led us on a walking tour of Prince Edward and Mong Kok. Win-win kept holding up his strawberry shake for me to take sips of, and I kept sharing my taro shake with him. The tour guide in me was charmed by the many themed streets and areas in Prince

Edward. There was Sneaker Street, which was nothing but stores selling sneakers from big brands like Nike and Adidas, and Ladies' Market, where I picked up a few magnets and keychains for my colleagues and relatives back home. Leo bargained hard and the stall owners ended up selling the trinkets to me for less than half the original asking price once they realized they were dealing with a local. To no one's surprise, Win-win's favorites were Goldfish Street, where every shop was filled with tanks of fish and reptiles, and egg cartons of crickets and other crawling insects to feed them with, and Pet Street, with its bunnies and hamsters. Most of the shop assistants were not particularly friendly, especially not when Win-win asked questions in Putonghua, but one took out a brown and white rabbit for Win-win to hold. 'Can we please have him, Mama?' Win-win pleaded.

'Someday,' I said, thankful that the shop assistant allowed Win-win to take a photo with the bunny before we had to go.

We walked for another two blocks or so before Leo announced, 'This is the flower market.' His expression was so hopeful; it was obvious that he was desperate for me to like it.

And I did, very much, more than I had liked any place in Hong Kong. It was tucked away behind the busiest thoroughfare of Prince Edward, an intersection of largely pedestrian-only roads crammed with florists and plant shops. Many of the stores had their metal shelves of potted plants and buckets of cut flowers overflowing onto the sidewalk, and everywhere people were stopping to admire the beauty of the flowers and breathe in their scent. Even the air seemed fresher and cleaner. It was marvelous.

'I love it,' I said, 'I've never been anywhere like it. I mean, there's the Botanical Garden back home, but you can't take any of the flowers home. 'This is amazing.'

'It's very nice,' Win-win chimed in, 'but not nearly so nice as Pet Street. Can we go back later to visit the bunny, Leo Shushu?'

'Sure,' Leo said. 'If it isn't too late. I was hoping your mom might help me pick out a few plants,' he said, shyly. 'You know how I only have one snake plant at home—' Here he grinned sheepishly, like a schoolboy admitting to some naughty deed. 'They're supposed to be impossible to kill, but I actually used to have three of them; two died on me. You only have to water them once a month, but sometimes I still forget. And sometimes I forget and water them twice.'

I loved him all the more for this confession. 'And you still want more?'

'You love plants so much.' He blushed a little. 'They make me think of you. And I...I want you to feel at home here, too.'

I reached out a hand to cup his stubbly chin. 'I'd love to help. I'm a real plant professional; you can count on me.'

As Leo and Win-win sat on a bench playing games on Leo's phone, I hurried in and out of several shops, studying their selections with pleasure. It didn't take me long to pick out two spider plants with sprawling, wispy tendrils—Leo could hang these up by his floor-to-ceiling windows. To these I added a Chinese Evergreen with vibrant green and pink leaves, each one the size of my hand. I eyed the volleyball-sized cactuses longingly, especially since they would match the lovely pendant had Leo bought me, but decided that they would be too tricky to transport back to Leo's apartment.

My final choice was a towering ZZ plant, one that reached to my waist. I've always loved plants with thick, waxy leaves, but the best part was that ZZ plants are known to be auspicious. Back home we called it the money tree. Pleased with my choice, I brought the plant to the cashier—I was fifth in line. I studied the orchids as I waited and decided the yellow and purple ones were the prettiest. Orchids could be finicky, though, not really for beginners. Anyway, Leo asked specifically for hardy plants.

'That will be $168, please,' the cashier said, interrupting my thoughts. She pushed back her sweaty bangs from her forehead. She was trying to smile but she kept looking past me at the growing line. 'Do you need a bag?'

I shook my head as I reached for the bills inside my wallet. To my dismay, however, there were only three fifty-dollar bills inside; I was short $18. In my excitement I must have lost track of how much money I spent on the other plants. I unzipped my shoulder bag as well—I was sure there were some coins at the bottom, perhaps a few five or ten-dollar coins. I could call Leo, but my hands were full, and I didn't want him to know that I barely had any cash left.

'Hurry up,' someone grumbled behind me. A few people murmured their agreement.

'We also take Octopus,' the cashier said, tapping the laminated poster beside the cash register. 'Visa. Mastercard.'

I didn't have any of those. I reached to the bottom of my handbag and scooped up the coins at the bottom. It was a good handful, I thought hopefully, but I held up the coins only to realize that they were all coins from home. 'We don't accept Renminbi,' the cashier said loudly, her smile gone. 'I'm going to have to help the next customer now. Please line up again when you're ready to pay.'

'Go back to where you came from, mainlander,' I heard someone sneer. I didn't dare look up to see who had said this. My cheeks burning with shame, I slunk to the back of the shop and returned the ZZ plant to the shelf. I should leave—but a stubborn part of me refused to give up—I reached for a smaller ZZ plant instead, about 10 inches tall, still lucky. This one was only $98.

I got back in line. My phone buzzed in my pocket but I forced myself to ignore it. I didn't want to hold up the line again.

I didn't make eye contact with the cashier when it was my

turn; I just handed over two of my fifty-dollar notes and grabbed the change without looking back.

'The line was quite long,' I said, by way of explanation, when I returned to Leo and Win-win at their bench. They scooted over to make room for me. I wanted to tell Leo what happened so I could be comforted. Dating Leo had spoiled me; I used to be so independent! But when I opened my mouth, ready to tell him about how I hadn't brought enough money, and how the people in the shop had been rude to me, I could anticipate his questions: *But why didn't you call me? Why didn't you just leave the plant behind?* I didn't really have any good answers. I had just sort of frozen up.

Instead, I presented the money tree to him with two hands. "This plant is supposed to bring you happiness and prosperity. I want you to have lots and lots of happiness, all the happiness in the world.' I wished it were the bigger plant. 'It's also very hardy, super easy to care for.'

'It's beautiful,' he said, touching the leaves appreciatively. 'But you know, I've never been as happy as I've been this week, with you.' He kissed me on the cheek. 'Even before you got me the plant.'

On our way back to the bus stop, we passed by a short, squat little building, only three or four stories tall, with the silver characters, *Golden Plaza*, over the entrance looking like they needed a good wipe down. Half a dozen or so middle-aged ladies were standing on the steps, handing out flyers with great enthusiasm. I managed to make my way past them empty-handed but Win-win ended up with a small handful. 'It's all wedding stuff,' I said, glancing at them. 'Dresses and wedding favours and things.' I pretended not to be interested — we had already talked about this and agreed that we'd revisit the idea of marriage later on, after we spent more time together in Hong

Kong. Such decisions could not be made so hastily, could they?

But Leo surprised me. 'If you want to, we can take a look inside.' He lowered his voice to a whisper. 'You would make such a pretty bride. I wish we could get married today.'

I blushed furiously. 'Don't joke about things like that. We said we'd wait—'

'I know.' Leo said, immediately penitent. 'I'm sorry. I'm just so in love with you.'

How could I be angry at that? I reached for my cactus pendant and stroked its prickly surface — the pricks coming from the little diamonds — until I felt more grounded.

'Let's just take a quick look,' I finally said. 'It'll be cooler inside, anyway.'

Using an app from his phone, Leo booked a van to pick up our plants and sent them home first so we wouldn't be weighed down with them while we walked around.

Once we were inside I realized we were in wedding heaven. The tiny mall was bursting at its seams with wedding vendors — the first floor was jam packed with little stores whose shopfronts were spilling over with their wares: gold and red teapots and embroidered kneeling cushions for the tea ceremony, silk corsages and boutonnieres of every style and color, and wedding favors — oh, the wedding favors! — from towels folded into roses and rabbits to wedding invitations printed onto wooden puzzles to tiny heart-shaped tins of tea.

Win-win pointed at the balloon shop in the corner, at the blinding silver and hot pink balloon arch over the doorway. When Leo nodded, Win-win ran over to it, holding up his hands in peace signs as Leo took pictures.

Dreamy classic love songs were playing over the loudspeakers, and everybody in the mall seemed to be humming the familiar tunes as they milled about, happily running their errands. It was wedding land.

'I thought we could look around,' Leo was saying, suddenly shy. 'If you want to, I mean.' He hesitated, and I knew he was thinking of the way I stopped him from buying souvenirs for us at Disneyland. 'No pressure, of course. Only if you want to.'

When I stood on my tiptoes and kissed him on the cheek, I could see—and feel—him visibly relax. He was right—it was far too early for any kind of wedding shopping—but it didn't hurt to look around.

The first store we stopped at was filled with wedding outfits in miniature: tiny suits and ties for boys, and frilly white and pink dresses, bouquets, hair accessories, and glittery shoes for the flower girls. The saleswoman urged Win-win to try on a charcoal five-piece ensemble, complete with a glossy satin bowtie and a handkerchief for the chest pocket, and I refused at first, because we had no intention of buying it, but the saleswoman assured us that there was no pressure. Win-win emerged from the tiny dressing room looking so darling, I couldn't take my eyes off him. How could I have considered refusing to let Win-win look this adorable?

I perched on Leo's knee, studying the pretty flower girl dresses with interest. I reached my hand out to touch the gauzy fabrics, wondering if they would feel scratchy against a little girl's skin. Win-win, back in his own shorts and T-shirt, returned to us.

'Ten percent off for you, best deal in Hong Kong,' the shop attendant said with an authoritative air. 'Cash or credit card?'

But I shook my head. 'We were just trying,' I protested, but I could already see the saleswoman's frown. I didn't want to buy the five-piece suit. It was clearly for a ringbearer, and there was as yet no wedding to wear it to. Maybe someday—but not today.

Instead, Leo chose several loud nylon ties—a neon orange, a striped red and green, several with leopard prints in different colors. They didn't suit him at all. He paid for them with a hundred-dollar bill and the lady packed them in a plastic bag covered in red hearts. 'I'll need a receipt, please,' he added. She scribbled something on a notepad and tore off the sheet for him.

'I didn't want the lady shouting at us for only looking and not buying anything,' he explained as we took the escalator. 'These will make good props for my Drama Club.'

The second floor was mostly wedding dress stores. Half of them featured Western style gowns, all lace and tulle and satin. To my untrained eye they seemed very flashy and over-the-top with their sprawling trains and deep-V necklines. I couldn't see myself wearing any of them. The other half was filled with elaborate *qun kua*, the luxurious, finely embroidered gold and red wedding costumes that women back home wore on their wedding day. Between the wedding dress stores there were also little shops that specialized in bridal undergarments — never had I seen so many silicone bra styles — and provocative lingerie for the wedding night. I quickly steered Win-win towards the escalator.

'Do you see anything you like?' Leo squeezed my hand as the third floor came into view. He told me last night that he was long overdue for a haircut, but I liked his hair this way, floppy and soft, almost like he was the senior member of a boy band. His appearance wasn't what attracted me to him first — but he *was* handsome. Very much so.

Win and I were one step higher than Leo was, putting me and Leo at exactly the same height, at eye level. 'Yes,' I said, slowly. 'I see you.'

I saw surprise register in his eyes, but he recovered quickly. Grinning slyly, he brushed his lips against mine, sending a jolt of desire through me. 'Do you, now,' he murmured.

I was about to respond when I suddenly heard Win-win shout,

A SUMMER LIKE THAT

'Mama, look out!' I felt him grabbing my dress and yanking me forward. He had stopped me from tripping on the top step of the escalator.

'Sorry, sorry,' Leo and I both muttered sheepishly. We exchanged a look over Win-win's head, one that said, *This is not over*.

The top floor was mostly filled with shops specializing in bridesmaid dresses and outfits for the mother of the bride and groom, but I also saw all kinds of vendors — photographers and videographers, invitation designers, make-up artists, venue decorators, wedding planners, bakers, florists, and more — advertising their services out of tiny, but lovingly decorated shops, often with just one member of staff.

The biggest and busiest shop on this floor was a shoe store with an auspicious name: *Lucky Shoes*. We hovered by the entrance, mesmerized by the busyness within. I'd never seen anything like it — all the shoes were custom order, and the grey-haired salesmen, dressed in faded navy trousers and white button-up shirts, were also shoemakers who added the details as their customers described them. One balding salesman held a plain red ballerina flat in one hand as his customer pointed to a white tub of gold sequins on the floor and gestured to the front of the shoe, where the toe box was. She gesticulated with her hands, pointing to images on her phone, until the salesman nodded and began attaching the sequins to the satin one-by-one with a stapler-like tool. Beside him, another salesman was swiftly attaching a large emerald to an ivory stiletto. It was all costume jewelry, of course, but still, it looked wonderfully glamorous.

'Go on, then,' Leo said, nudging me forward. 'Took a look inside.'

Leo and Win-win sat down on one of the aging pleather couches to play a game together on Leo's phone as I started looking around. There was a very large selection of shoes here, some modern styles, and some which were clearly targeted at older women.

One pair caught my eye immediately — it had the shimmery, translucent sheen of a moonstone or cat's eye, or maybe glass under the light of the moon. They brought to mind Cinderella's glass slippers, and although our tight budget meant that I'd learned not to take much interest in shoe or handbag shopping — I found these shoes irresistible. They looked like they belonged in a fairy tale ending. *And*, I told myself, *they could be pretty just for going out in, not just for a wedding.* They were $229, not cheap, but not unthinkable, either.

'I'd like to try this pair, please,' I heard myself saying as one of the salesmen approached me.

He nodded. Without speaking, he measured my left foot on the yellowing plastic gauge before promptly returning with a pair of the Cinderella shoes in my size. I slipped them on and stood before the angled floor mirror. The shoes only pinched a little, and they made my feet look slimmer and daintier than they were.

'Those are pretty, Mama,' Win-win said, glancing up from Leo's phone. They were playing a two-player racing game, their four hands grabbing the four corners of the smart phone at once.

'Very pretty,' Leo agreed.

'Would you like to add any accessories, ma'am?' The salesman gestures towards the tubs at our feet. 'Sequins, pearls, bows, beads, anything you want—'

Leo tapped at his phone before handing it to Win-win. 'Try single-player mode now,' he said. 'Remember to use the turbo mode on the highway.'

'Yes, sir!' Win-win cried.

Leo reached into the tub of pearls and held out several

ornaments, but it wasn't until he dug out a bow-like pearl ornament with three pearls—two big ones flanking a smaller one in between—that we both nodded. 'This one's you,' I whispered, kissing the top of Win-win's head. 'My baby pearl.'

He nodded absently, glancing at the pearls for the briefest of moments before returning to his race.

The salesman held it against the front of the shoe and waited for my okay before gluing it down. He set it down to dry before raking through the tub with his wrinkled fingers. He had to be in his seventies. 'And here's its twin,' he said, swiftly attaching the matching ornament to the other shoe.

'Let me buy these for you,' Leo said, holding out his credit card to the cashier before I could protest. 'As thanks for your help with the plants,' he added hastily. 'And because you look so pretty in them. And because I love you.' We were sent outside to wait while the glue dried.

'I think it's time for a snack,' Leo declared. We took the escalators back down to the ground floor and left the mall. 'What does everyone feel like? Waffles? Steamed milk pudding? Macaroni with beef? Pineapple buns?'

Win-win wanted the pudding and Leo and I wanted the macaroni, so Leo took us to the bustling Yee Shun Dairy Company, where tourists and locals alike were scarfing down their specialties. Win-win declared the milk pudding the tastiest thing he'd ever had in his life. 'It's even better than ice cream, Ah Meh!' he cried in the video recording I sent to Ma.

The moment we finished our food, our bowls were cleared away, a strong hint that we should leave to make room for the next patrons.

As we headed back up to Lucky Shoes, a dress in the window of one of the bridesmaid dress shops caught my eye. 'Can we go back down?' I ask. 'I...I thought I saw—'

'Of course,' Leo said, taking both our hands, one in each of his.

The three of us stood in front of the store. I pressed my hands against the window, studying the dress. Having seen the over-the-top bridal gowns from the first floor, I knew that this cream floor-length dress was clearly designed with a bridesmaid in mind. But it was so beautiful, quietly elegant, with dainty lace cap sleeves and a ruched empire waist.

The shop attendant popped her head out. 'Want to try it on? This is the latest. The changing room is tiny, but I can help you—'

'Not today,' I said, slipping my hand in Leo's. The shoes I could justify—but it was really too soon to be buying a dress. 'Thank you, though.'

Chapter 22
Leo

Just before we left Prince Edward, we passed by a traditional bedding shop, the kind that sold bed linens, pillows, and custom-cut foam mattresses. I asked Pearl and Win-win to wait outside. 'I'll just be a minute,' I promised.

I pulled out my phone, ignoring the texts from Henry, my mother, and to my dismay, Lindsay again, and tapped impatiently on the Google Drive icon. I had all the paperwork from when I was having renovations done, including measurements of all the rooms and custom-built furniture.

Lindsay used to laugh at me for being so organized. 'Stop being so OCD,' she used to tease, but no amount of teasing could stop me from scanning everything — from my initial sketches and ideas to inspiration from websites and furniture catalogues, and eventually, the receipts from all the purchases. To Lindsay's great amusement, I had every item arranged by date and category, and assigned to a color-coded folder.

A quick glance at my living room dimensions showed me that when the futon at home was laid out on the floor beside the loveseat, the remaining gap was just under two feet wide. It was unlikely, but not impossible, that a shop like this would sell a mattress that narrow.

'What're you looking for?' A curly-haired woman about my mother's age peered at me from behind the scratched glass counter. 'You're so handsome, exactly like my son! He's in England, you know, studying to be a doctor. For a handsome man like you, 20% discount!'

'I want to buy a mattress,' I began, glancing around the dimly lit shop. Even though everything looked clean, it also looked as though it had all been here since the eighties, or earlier. Even my grandmother would find the designs on some of these bed linens old-fashioned. That reminded me—I needed to choose a present for Grandma before her birthday dinner the day after tomorrow. If not a present, then at least a cash gift—either would do.

It turned out they did carry 23-inch mattresses. 'Lots of custom orders that people end up forgetting about,' the woman explained, shrugging. 'We have every size, and anything we don't have, we can make for you within two business days.' She held up her fingers in a peace sign as she said this. She studied my face thoughtfully before proclaiming, 'I think you might be handsome enough for a 25% discount!'

'Thank you,' I said absently. 'I'll take that one,' I said, pointing at the mattress whose plastic cover was the least yellowed.

She rolled up the mattress with surprising speed and ease, tying a length of purple nylon string around its girth to form a handle.

At the last moment I chose a king-sized bedsheet, a plain beige one, and got 25% off on that too. I left the shop to the woman's jubilant cries of 'Goodbye, handsome man, goodbye!'

———∽∾∽———

After getting home from Prince Edward, we unfolded my old

futon and uncurled the new mattress, laying them out side by side in the living room before wrapping the new bedsheet around them both. It was a snug and altogether perfect fit; I found it very satisfying that all my measurements were correct. The three of us watched *Toy Story 3* sprawled out on the floor. Win-win clutched both Simba and Wuwu anxiously to his chest for the entirety of the film, his eyes wide with worry for the welfare of Andy's toys.

The living room grew dark around us as night fell. I ordered takeout for dinner as Pearl and Win-win sniffled through that last tearjerker of a scene with Andy introducing Bonnie to his beloved toys. Afterwards, as we ate stuffed-crust pizza and fried chicken, our faces gleaming with grease and happiness, Win-win cried, 'I'm so happy!'

Win-win fell asleep almost immediately after his bath. I thought of Corrie, who liked to stay up till midnight sometimes 'just to see what it's like to be a real princess'. Thoughts of Corrie naturally led to thoughts of her father, whose messages I needed to attend to. I resolved to send Henry a reply a bit later.

While Pearl was in the shower, I carefully clipped up two bedsheets to my retractable clothing line to form a sort of makeshift tent. I switched off all the lights except the lamp at the foot of the loveseat so the living room was bathed in a warm, campfire-like glow. It was so cheesy, but knowing Pearl, I was certain she'd appreciate my efforts. I was sitting cross-legged within the tent, adding the finishing touch—tapping on *My Heart Will Go On* in Apple Music—just as she emerged from the washroom, a towel around her shoulders.

I expected her face to light up, for her to laugh, as the tin whistle played its familiar and fittingly cheesy tune in the opening bars, but Pearl just stood there, blinking furiously. She was trying not to cry.

'Hey,' I said. I stuck my head out between the sheets and hold out my hand. 'Don't cry, love. Come inside.'

She crawled in and snuggled up next to me. She was warm from her shower, her cheeks hot and flushed, and she smelled like the Johnson's baby wash I bought for Win-win.

'It's cozy in here,' she whispered, wiping her eyes with the heel of her hand. 'It's fun.'

When I lay down, Pearl joined me, fitting her backside snugly against my tummy, and it felt like we were teenagers at high school camp. I draped my arm around her waist, drawing her even closer. We listened to the soundtrack together like this for several minutes, relishing the closeness.

Just as my desire for her was reaching its peak, she tilted her head up towards me and murmured, 'Leo, I want you.'

I leaned in to kiss her on the side of her neck and she let out a quiet sigh of pleasure. 'More, please,' she whispered.

I was more than happy to oblige.

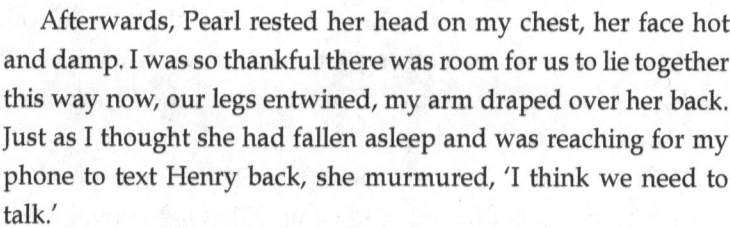

Afterwards, Pearl rested her head on my chest, her face hot and damp. I was so thankful there was room for us to lie together this way now, our legs entwined, my arm draped over her back. Just as I thought she had fallen asleep and was reaching for my phone to text Henry back, she murmured, 'I think we need to talk.'

Immediately I felt my body tense, the old fear creeping back. 'Okay,' I said, my heart hammering in my chest. I tried my best not to sound alarmed, but it was so hard. The last time someone said *I think we need to talk* to me, she was breaking up with me. 'W-what do you want to talk about?' I hoped she didn't notice the tremor in my voice.

She did, though, I'm sure she did, because she wriggled around to face me and stroked my cheek with her hand. 'Hey,' she said tenderly. 'I love you. I was just thinking...worrying... about your parents. Are you sure they're not going to try and stop us from being together?' This came out in a rush, as though she had been wanting to ask me this question for a long time. 'In my village, if the parents don't approve of a match, they'll do everything in their power to break it up.' She hesitated. 'I mean, with Win-win's father, my mother didn't find out until it was too late, but...if she'd known, things would have ended up differently for sure.'

'I'm sorry that man hurt you,' I said, softly, 'but this is different. My mom can be pretty hot-tempered in the heat of things, but my parents have been harping on me to settle down for years.'

Pearl looked up at me uncertainly. 'I don't think I'm the kind of woman your parents were hoping you'd choose to settle down with. Your mother mentioned...some concerns about mainlanders—'

'Come on, love,' I pleaded. 'Let me worry about my parents. They'll come around; I promise.'

'Maybe,' she said, sounding unconvinced. 'Maybe you should go to your grandma's party on Sunday without us. It feels too soon for you to be introducing me to all your relatives.' She hesitated. 'You're not upset?'

'Of course not.' Quite the contrary—I was trying not to show how relieved I felt. I hadn't worked out what I was going to do about Grandma's dinner—Pearl and Win-win would have felt awkward and out-of-place among my relatives, there was no doubt about that. This way they would be safe at home, free from my nosy and judgmental family's uncomfortable questions. This was definitely for the best.

'And you know, we've been talking about our coming here to live with you...so Win and I should probably head back to Xiamen to sort things out. I know Ma's going to be so happy for us, but it'll still be an adjustment for her to live on her own.' Without any warning at all, her eyes welled up with tears. 'We've been like peanuts in a pod practically since I was born.'

'Of course,' I said, softly. 'I'm asking a lot of you. If you want, I could try and find work in Xiamen.' It wouldn't be easy, but it wasn't impossible. Might there be an international school or language centre I could teach at? In my mind I ran through the job search websites for mainland China that I was aware of. I could do a quick search tonight after Pearl and Win-win were asleep. 'That way you could stay home, and we could still—'

'Silly,' she said, laughing through her tears. 'We couldn't do that to you. You're already sharing so much with us—your space, your privacy, your *life*...Anyway, it'll be good for Win-win to learn Cantonese and English, and everything. I'm glad we're coming.' She let out a watery laugh. 'I'm just going to miss Ma, is all. But she'll only be a few hours away.'

I kissed her on the forehead. 'You're right. Only a few hours, not far at all.'

Chapter 23
Pearl

The next morning, after breakfast Leo invited us for a walk around the neighborhood. It was a warm, sunny Saturday; lots of people were jogging, walking their dogs, soaking up the good weather. I was pleased to see that in our shorts and T-shirts, we fitted right in. The three of us walked hand in hand, Win-win skipping between us, carefully avoiding the red tiles in the sidewalk. 'Win is four and a half,' Leo said, 'which means —'

'*Nearly* five, Leo Shushu.' Win-win corrected him. 'Mama said I'll be five in October. That's soon, isn't it?'

I glanced at Leo, whose expression was so full of affection for my son, and then at Win-win, who seemed to be so comfortable with Leo and in this environment, here in Hong Kong. It all felt too good to be true — like I'd picked up a winning lottery ticket off the ground, but any moment now someone would be after me to get it back. *You put that down! That's not yours!*

'Very soon,' Leo agreed. 'Win's nearly five, which means that he'll be starting K2 in a few weeks, on September 1.' He stopped walking and pointed to the grey building across the street; it was a short one by Hong Kong standards, just five storeys. He had a curious expression on his face, halfway between sheepish and playful, one I had come to recognize as the preamble to a surprise. 'There's a kindergarten on the top floor of that building. I...called ahead and asked if it would be alright for us to visit today.' He paused, squeezing my hand. 'You want to take a look inside?'

We hadn't talked about Win-win's schooling too much, even though privately, I had been trying to do some research on the Internet to find out as much as I could. My efforts had mostly been fruitless, though—with my very limited knowledge of Hong Kong's parenting forums, I couldn't find much. A lot of the so-called information seemed to be little more than speculation or hearsay, and none of it seemed to be about Leo's neighborhood here in Sham Tseng. I should have just asked Leo, of course—he was a teacher himself, after all—but I was shy about bringing up the topic with him. I just didn't want to overwhelm him with one more problem to worry about.

I was keenly aware of how much and how quickly Leo's life was changing because of us. His home used to be like a show home, it was so sleek and stylish. Even the books on his shelf were organized by color; I had never seen anything like it. But now our things were everywhere: rattan baskets of toys here, a stack of folded clothing there, our toiletries, our shoes, our suitcases. Try as I might to keep things tidy, the truth was that the stuff itself, no matter how tidily stacked or folded, was making his sleek home feel crowded and busy. He kept telling us how much he loved us, but sometimes I wondered if we ourselves were crowding up his home, too. 'Yes, please,' I finally said. 'Thank you so much.'

Leo walked between us, taking both of our hands and leading us into the rather dimly lit lobby of the building. 'It's on the top floor,' he said, pressing the '5' on the elevator button panel.

'Will there be children there today, Leo Shushu?' Win-win asked, a slight frown on his face.

'I don't think so,' Leo said, giving Win's shoulder a little squeeze. 'It's still summer. But the principal will be there; I told her I was bringing a very special little boy to visit today.'

Win-win giggled. 'That's me.'

When the doors slid open my eyes were immediately drawn to the wall of hanging plants — it cheered me to see so much greenery, and so well cared-for, and in the corner there was an enormous fish tank with tropical fish swimming to and fro. A lot of the decor appeared to have been crafted out of construction paper and paper mache, from the enormous rainbow tree by the entrance to the friendly jungle creatures — a sloth, a cheetah, a monkey — suspended from the ceiling. There was children's artwork everywhere — framed paintings and drawings on the walls, little clay sculptures on the window sills, shoebox dioramas on top of the cabinets.

The beaming woman who stood to greet us looked like she was probably in her mid-forties. Dressed in a striped black and white blouse, denim pinafore with enormous heart-shaped pockets, and red tights, she looked so confident and attractive, she could be a kindergarten teacher in a movie. Her hair was in two buns secured with red ribbons, a style that might have looked silly and childish on anyone else, but somehow worked on her and made her look even more like a model kindergarten teacher. Back at my workplace in Xiamen, all the teachers and assistants had to wear the same ugly pink and grey uniform.

'You must be Win-win's family!' Her Cantonese sounded like music. 'I'm the principal here; you can call me Miss Penny. Welcome to Sham Tseng Nursery School!'

Win-win, normally so loquacious, immediately buried his head against my leg. I wanted to say something in response — but

I wasn't sure if Miss Penny understood Putonghua, and my own Cantonese was so heavily accented, I couldn't be sure if she'd understand that either. As I was deliberating between the two, Leo came to our rescue. 'It's a pleasure to meet you, Miss Penny,' he said in Putonghua. His Putonghua had improved so much compared to just a few weeks ago. When he smiled at us, I felt how proud he was of us, despite everything. I felt myself drawing strength from his confidence, and managed a small smile. 'Win-win is new to Hong Kong, and still picking up Cantonese.'

'No problem,' Miss Penny said, switching smoothly into Putonghua. 'It's so nice to meet you, Win-win,' she tried again, crouching in front of Win. 'Thank you for visiting today.'

She spoke so gently, so sincerely, that Win-win couldn't help but turn around and greet her. '*Nihao*, Miss Penny,' he whispered. 'It's nice to meet you, too.'

She reached into one of her heart-shaped pockets and took out a green smiley-face sticker. 'This is for you, Win-win,' she said, placing it in his hand. 'The shop owner said if I scratched it, it would smell like something yummy! Can you help me?'

He began scratching at the sticker with his index finger in earnest before holding it up to his nose. 'Nothing yet,' he murmured, before scratching it some more and sniffing at it again. He did this with the focus of a scientist on the verge of a breakthrough. 'It smells like candy,' he finally said. 'Maybe apple candy, but I'm not very sure.'

'Apple candy! Of course! *That's* what it was.' Miss Penny exclaimed, acting so grateful and impressed, I wasn't surprised at all when Win-win allowed her to hold his hand.

As Miss Penny showed us around the kindergarten, we saw that there were, as Leo predicted, no other children at school, just a few teachers getting things ready for the new school year. Miss Penny was very intentional about introducing Win-win to each teacher as we walked along; each one greeted him warmly. I could see the bounce in his step returning. She highlighted to him the features of the various classrooms but did so in a gentle, child-friendly way — he looked curious and interested rather than overwhelmed.

Leo and I walked behind them, listening. The classrooms were a good size, spacious and inviting, with large windows that let in a good deal of light. In the K1 classroom, two teachers were constructing an elaborate bakery corner, with a delightfully realistic sliding display cabinet filled with construction paper pastries. On top of the counter were several pairs of plastic tongs, a toy cashier with an octopus card reader, and a stack of small brown paper bags. Behind the counter there were red and white aprons hanging on a hook.

'And this here is our library,' Miss Penny said, leading us into a smaller room at the end of the hallway. It was filled, floor to ceiling, with books. There was a pair of child-sized armchairs in one corner, a stack of fluffy floor cushions in another. In my mind's eye I could see Win-win curling up in one of those armchairs and enjoying a storybook. I wasn't much of a reader myself, but I thought of Leo sprawled on the sofa, his brows furrowed as he read a novel. It would be marvelous if one day Win-win could end up like that too, a bookworm.

'I have one last area to show you,' she said, leading us up a flight of stairs. The door opened to reveal an inviting rooftop play area with swings, slides, a climbing frame, and even sand and water play areas. Win-win would have so much fun here.

'What do you think?' Leo whispered, drawing me close for a kiss on the cheek. 'Do you like it?'

I turned to face him, opening my mouth to respond, but I was distracted by the sight of Win-win, who was ahead of us, with Miss Penny. When she gestured at the green slide, his eyes lit up.

JANE LO

It was quite tall, maybe twice Leo's height, but Win-win climbed up the ladder with ease, like a little monkey. I felt a surge of pride at how nimble, how agile my son was even in this unfamiliar environment. 'It's such a lovely school.'

Leo smiled. 'I think so, too. We can explore other places, too. There's —'

'But will they accept him?' I had so many questions. 'Win-win doesn't speak any Cantonese yet. Or English. There'll be an interview, won't there? How will Win-win manage? And…how much will it cost for him to study here? Is it even legal for him to —'

'Hey,' Leo said quietly. 'Give me those.' He reached for my hands, unfurled them to reveal the half-moons on my palms where my nails had dug in. Out of the corner of my eye I could see Miss Penny showing Win-win a wall covered with interconnected wooden gears. When Win reached out his hand to turn the handle, the whole wall came to life.

'Leo, I—'

'You aren't on your own anymore,' he said, wrapping his arms around me. He held me so close that I couldn't help but close my eyes as I rested my head against his chest. His T-shirt smelled like Dettol, a clean, fresh scent I now associated with home. 'We'll work it out together. The principal said she has one or two spots left in K3, and promised to think about admitting Win-win.'

I gasp. 'You mean that was the interview? We didn't prepare —'

'Not an official interview,' Leo said quickly. 'Don't worry. But the principal told me on the phone that she'd be happy to accept a few more children, and why wouldn't anyone want Win-win? He's the best-behaved little boy in the world, no question about that. And you don't have to worry about the cost, I —'

I had my doubts about whether any school would consider

accepting my son, who would be like a fish out of water in a fully Cantonese and English environment. It was true that the principal spoke Putonghua, but what about the children? The other teachers? And how could I let Leo pay for everything, even Win-win's tuition fees? I was already shaking my head. 'No, I—'

'Please,' he said, his eyes bright with sincerity, 'we can work it out together. I would be happy to cover the cost. *More* than happy. All I want—' here he paused, his voice thick with emotion, 'Pearl, all I want is for you to be happy.'

*

After our visit to the kindergarten, we went to a Korean barbecue restaurant in Tsing Yi for lunch. 'It's all you can eat,' Leo explained, bringing us on a tour of the restaurant and showing us the different sections of the buffet: marinated meat, cooked dishes, desserts, a salad bar, and an extensive drinks selection that reminded me of being at 7-11. 'It's a buffet, so you can choose whatever you like.'

Win-win clapped in delight. 'I'll go get the drinks!'

We probably had buffet-style restaurants like this in Xiamen, but Win-win and I had never been to one. I quickly busied myself with getting slices of marinated beef, pork, and chicken to grill at our table while Win-win piled up his dish with fried chicken wings, fried rice, and French fries.

'This place is the *best*,' Win-win declared, sitting down and reaching for a fry. 'There's ice cream, *six* flavors, over there.'

It made me smile to see Leo cooking for us, arranging the meat in neat concentric circles on the grill with the tongs. 'It's my turn to cook for you,' he said, proudly. He placed a glistening piece of beef in my bowl. 'Here, try this first. The wings take a bit longer. Want a sausage, Win?'

'No, thank you,' Win said, smiling from ear to ear as he buried another fry in ketchup. 'Can I go get some mango pudding,

JANE LO

Mama?'

When he returned, he was holding a dessert bowl of mango pudding with bits of real mango in it, and drenched in evaporated milk. 'The lady helped me with the milk,' he said, beaming. 'Leo Shushu, did you know, I *love* mango pudding!'

Leo was about to open his mouth and respond when his phone clattered against the table. *DAD*, it said. Frowning, Leo handed me the metal tongs. 'Can you take over for a minute?'

I nodded, trying my best to smile and look reassuring as Leo said, 'Hello, Dad?'

'Yes, they are,' he continued, his brow furrowed. But soon I was not able to keep up with the English conversation. I removed the cooked chicken wings from the grill and arranged them in a little stack on Leo's plate. Win-win held up a spoonful of mango pudding to me and I ate it, but I had lost my appetite.

Finally, Leo hung up. 'Sorry about that. My parents invited us to their home for dinner tonight.' He sighed. 'My brother's family is going to be there, too. We don't have to go if you don't want to. I told my dad I'll call him back to let him know.'

This sounded stressful, even worse than his grandma's birthday party would have been. At a restaurant, in a large crowd of relatives, we could have stayed relatively invisible, but at Leo's parents' home we would be expected to make conversation and answer questions. And if Leo's dad and brother were anything like his mother and sister-in-law, it wasn't going to be a very pleasant evening at all. But I could see that Leo was pleading with me to say yes. I reached for the cactus pendant at my neck and stroked its grooved underside. *You jump, I jump*, I imagined reading with the pad of my thumb. 'It's very kind of them to invite us,' I said, carefully. 'I think we should go.'

Leo stabbed one of the chicken wings with his chopsticks. 'Yes, but if you —'

A SUMMER LIKE THAT

'What kind of fruit do your parents like?' I interrupted, hoping that my mother's mantra of *courtesy opens doors* would ring true here in Hong Kong as well as it did in Xiamen. 'Can I buy them some?'

———∞———

I checked my appearance one last time in the elevator. Wearing this peachy shirt dress—it looked so good on the model in the Taobao ad, she had styled it with these high-top sneakers and a hairband that made her look like a Korean popstar—was a mistake; the dark patches around the neckline and under the arms were very unsightly. Stuffing my neck fan into my purse, I slipped between the elevator doors just as they were closing. We were on the highest floor of the building, the 38th.

In my hands, in one of Leo's cloth shopping bags, were the vegetables Ma insisted I bring, the cauliflower and carrots from the fields, as well as the fruits Leo said were his parents' favorites: two pounds of eye-wateringly expensive Japanese grapes for his mom, and six enormous golden kiwis for his dad. At the last moment I had added a large tray of Korean strawberries—not cheap, but a good size and nicely packaged—for the children. Leo said his brother, sister-in-law, and niece would be at dinner, too. Leo offered to pay for the fruit, but of course I wouldn't let him—I wouldn't even let him carry them for me. I needed his parents to see my sincerity.

Leo stopped in front of Flats C and D—two flats that shared an imposing oversized door of dark wood. A bronze plaque with stylized Chinese characters hung upon the door: *God is the Head of this House.* I glanced at him, surprised. 'You believe in God?'

He shrugged. 'My parents do.' He scooped Win-win up to ring the doorbell.

'Remember to greet everyone, Win,' I murmured, although I

knew he would. 'Remember not to reach across the table or talk with your mouth full. No elbows on the table.'

Win-win, who was humming along to the doorbell tune, held up both thumbs.

Leo slipped his hand into mine as we heard slippered feet padding towards the door. 'I love you,' he whispered. 'Everything will be fine.'

Leo's mom and dad opened the door together. We were welcomed into the flat, and I nodded and smiled as we handed them the fruits and vegetables, removed our shoes, and shook hands, but in the first few seconds I was so taken aback by their living room that I could barely speak. It was an overwhelmingly large space—maybe four times bigger than Leo's entire flat, and very luxuriously outfitted. Each of the two chandeliers was made up of what looked like hundreds of tear-drop shaped crystals; the effect was impressive but also dizzying. In the dining area to the left of the living room was an oval marble dining table surrounded by eight intricately carved wooden chairs. A cylindrical glass vase of perhaps two dozen pink roses sat at the centre of the table. I felt like I was on a television set. Fresh flowers! The pinnacle of luxury. Rivulets of sweat trickled down the sides of my face. How I wished I could put my neck fan back on.

With a start I realized Leo was squeezing my hand. His father was speaking to me.

'You must be Pearl,' he said in lightly accented Putonghua, probably for the second time, but he didn't seem annoyed. Like Leo's, his smile was kind and warm. 'It's so nice to finally meet you and meet—' here he crouched so he was at eye-level with Win-win, 'this handsome boy.' He held out a closed fist to Win-win, a twinkle in his eye. 'I've got some sweets for you. If you can get them, you can have them. Want to try?'

A SUMMER LIKE THAT

Win-win tugged on my hand for permission. I nodded.

After a moment's thought, Win tickled the inside of Leo's father's wrist with his index finger, making him laugh in surprise and loosen his grip. Win-win swiftly grabbed the five Sugus candies from the palm of his hand. Each one was a different color. 'Well done! Clever boy!' Leo's father cried. 'They're all for you.'

'Thank you, Shushu,' Win-win said, shyly, bowing his head. With his left hand, he picked out the purple one, then returned the others. 'One is enough for me.'

'You are a very good boy,' his dad said, smiling. 'So polite! They really are all for you. You can save some for later if you want. Tell me, how —'

'Now, now, come say hello to me, too, Win-win.' Leo's mother interrupted, forced cheeriness in her voice. Seated on one of the ornate dining chairs, she reminded me of a queen dowager. She beckoned him over to her with her manicured index finger. 'Come here.'

As Leo led Win-win towards his mother, his dad lowered his voice: 'Our Corrie would have taken all five and then asked for five more.' Although he rolled his eyes as he said this, his affection for his granddaughter was unmistakable.

Out of the corner of my eye, I could see that Win-win was still sandwiched between Leo and his mother. Leo's mother's Putonghua was slightly better than his, and she fired her questions at Win-win like a rifle: *What is your name? How old are you? Where are you from? What do you like to read? What do you like to play?* As he answered, his voice was clear and sweet, and not hesitant at all. He kept his head bowed, the way he had been taught to do at school when speaking to any adult, especially when he was meeting them for the first time. I was thankful for the way Leo was keeping his hand on Win-win's shoulder, the way he was nodding and smiling at Win-win as he spoke.

Just then I saw Corrie—her hair in an elaborate braid that wrapped around her head like a crown—poke her head out of one of the rooms. 'What are *they* doing here, Yeh Yeh?' She said this in Cantonese, but it would have sounded disrespectful in any language.

'Come say hello,' her grandfather said, holding out his hand to her. 'Come, Corrie.'

She did, unwillingly, dragging her feet. She was wearing a buttery yellow princess dress, the outfit made complete with a strand of clear yellow beads around her neck and shimmery yellow nail polish.

'I remember *you*,' she said, scowling. 'I saw you at Disneyland with Uncle Leo.'

'Good memory,' I said, gently, in Putonghua. 'It's so nice to—'

But she interrupted me: 'I don't know what she's saying! I don't know what she's saying!'

'Why, Corrie,' her grandfather said, frowning. 'That's not very—'

Behind us, the doorbell rang again. Leo's mother jumped up at once. 'That must be Henry and Melissa!' she cried, beaming. She opened the door at the same time that Corrie disappeared into the room she had come from. In her stockinged feet, her steps were almost silent.

'Hi Nai Nai! Hi Lo Yeh!' Leo's sister-in-law cried, embracing them both as though they were good friends. She was as beautiful as I remembered, her hair permed in that trendy Korean style—bangs at the front, wavy in the back. Her makeup was so well-applied that it looked like she wasn't wearing any at all, and she just had flawless, dewy skin naturally. I tried not to slink to the back, newly ashamed of my own hair and face. My nose was peeling a bit from being in the sun so much.

Behind her was a man who had to be Leo's older brother,

Henry. The two brothers looked alike, but Henry was paler and thinner, his wire-rimmed glasses giving him a serious, almost professorial look. He was struggling under the weight of an enormous cellophane-wrapped rattan basket of fruit. My heart sank; my small red bag of fruit wasn't going to impress anybody after all. Leo rushed over to help him with it, and together they brought it to the coffee table. Melissa gestured to the basket as she stepped daintily out of her flats. 'Lo Yeh, we got some fruit for you and Nai Nai. There was a special at Yata today, and everything looked *so* fresh—we just couldn't resist picking up a few things for you!'

'How kind of you,' Leo's dad said, smiling. 'Henry, Melissa—I'm not sure if you've met—'

'Your daughter-in-law sure knows what you like,' Leo's mom interrupted. 'We're *so* lucky, aren't we, honey?' Leo's dad nodded. 'Just look at all this—*all* your favorites, and mine, too. These grapes are enormous, Melissa—'

Leo cleared his throat as he joined me on the sofa. 'Henry, this is Pearl, my girlfriend, and her son, Win-win. Win, we bumped into Auntie Melissa at Disneyland, do you remember that?'

Win-win nodded. 'Hello, Melissa Yiyi. Hello, Henry Shushu,' he said in Putonghua.

Henry leaned over to whisper something in English, which I didn't understand, to his brother. Leo responded in Cantonese, for my benefit: 'Of course he can. He can understand Cantonese perfectly.'

Seemingly out of nowhere, something yellow crashed into Melissa, causing her to nearly fall over. It was Corrie. 'Mommy!' she cried. Melissa laughed, everyone laughed, as though this was adorable.

Behind us, a domestic helper in a striped apron was transferring steaming dishes, two by two, from the kitchen to the dining table. 'Time to eat!' Leo's mother announced. 'Gather around, everyone. Corrie, go wash your hands.'

'Win-win, you too,' Leo said, gently, nudging Win-win forward. 'The bathroom's that way.'

There were two children's dishes at the end of the table, one pink and the other purple, with Disney princess designs on them. 'Win-win can use the purple one,' Leo said, kissing me on the cheek. He lowered his voice. 'You doing okay?'

I tried to smile.

He placed a bit of everything into the little divided compartments of the plate, and set it in the spot between us. The helper had laid out a children's placemat with matching cutlery, also princess-themed. When Win-win returned from the bathroom, I noticed that his hair and the front of his shirt were a bit wet, but before I could comment, Leo's father began leading everyone in a pre-meal prayer.

'Let's bow our heads,' Leo's father said, in Putonghua. He smiled kindly at us. 'Please join us, Pearl and Win-win.' He folded his hands and closed his eyes, and everyone at the table, even Corrie, did the same.

His Putonghua was not perfect, but I was touched that he prayed in Putonghua, for our benefit: *Father in the sky, we thank you for this good food. We thank you for our family and friends. Help us to treat others with grace and kindness, the way you treat us...*

I was no stranger to spiritual matters—I had been assisting Ma with the offerings at our altar since I was a little girl—but this was the first time I had ever prayed like this. I wondered, idly, what Ma would say if I was ever to believe in the same god, and talk to him like this before meals, as though he was sitting here with us. Surely this god had little to do with *our* gods, the ones that belonged to our village and ancestors. I wasn't sure though. Before I had worked out all the connections between the two belief systems, everyone was saying 'Amen' and reaching for the serving spoons and chopsticks. For several moments, the only sounds in the expansive space were chopsticks against china and the muted sounds of chewing.

'Did everybody see the news about the parallel traders?' Melissa suddenly said, breaking the silence. 'Mainlanders are still crossing the border into Hong Kong to buy up formula and resell them once they're back in the mainland. At this rate, there won't be any formula left for *our* babies.'

'Is that right?' Leo's mom frowned, shaking her head. 'I'm glad things weren't like that when Corrie was born. Imagine making a profit from baby formula. So greedy and heartless, it's unbelievable.'

How I wished they would talk about something else. I tried not to think of Ma's text message from this morning, the one asking me to bring back some formula for Xiaobei. I wasn't going to sell it, though, so I wasn't in the same camp as these parallel traders Melissa was describing with such contempt. Or was I? Ma did ask me to bring back as many cans as I could...

'Maybe the formula they're buying is for their own families,' Leo said quietly, glancing at me. I was startled; it was as if he had read my mind. 'I mean, if the formula *here* was contaminated with melamine, you'd do anything to find a safe alternative for Corrie, wouldn't you? Even it meant going across the border?'

It meant the world to hear Leo standing up for me in this way. I hoped it would be enough for someone to change the topic.

But Melissa was shaking her head, clearly unconvinced. 'Don't be so naïve. I'll bet like, 99% of the mainland buyers are parallel traders. They *are* looking to turn a profit.' She turned to her husband, a belligerent expression on her face. '*Aren't* they, honey?'

'I suppose so,' Henry said dutifully, as he placed a piece

of barbecued pork in Corrie's bowl, but he didn't sound very convinced. 'Anyway–'

'It's not just the formula, either,' Melissa interrupted. 'It's the hospital beds. Pregnant women are still rushing across the Hong Kong border as they are in labour so the emergency rooms can't turn them away. That's a pretty underhanded way of getting the right of abode for their kids, don't you think?'

Is that what they thought of me, too? Was being in love with their brother an underhanded way of bringing my son to Hong Kong? The scent of those roses, all two dozen of them, suddenly seemed cloying, heavy. Leo refilled my cup with tea and I gratefully took a sip. It was Iron Buddha, the kind we drank at home, but bitter.

The domestic helper brought out one final dish, a glistening steamed fish covered with chopped scallions, cilantro, and ginger.

'Thank you, Lorna,' Leo's mom said in English. 'It must be tough for the hospital staff, having to deal with all these mainland patients...Do you need help, Corrie?'

Corrie had reached across the table with her chopsticks and started poking at the steamed fish. 'Got it,' she crowed, having extracted the tenderest part of the fish, the cheek, from the fish head. She popped it into her mouth. 'Yummy!'

Everyone laughed appreciatively at her cleverness. I glanced at Win-win, who had been eating the rice on his dish in silence. 'Want some fish?' I murmured, in our dialect. Win-win loved fish, but back home we usually pan-fried our fish so that it could be kept for several meals; a steamed fish had to be finished all at once.

Leo's dad flipped the fish over. He did it so gracefully, silently, without a single drop of soy sauce splashing onto the table. He poked out the other cheek with his chopsticks. Out of the corner of my eye I saw Leo's mother picking up her bowl as though she was preparing to accept it. To everyone's surprise, he placed the fish cheek on Win-win's dish, on top of his half-eaten rice. 'This is the tastiest part, Win-win,' he said in Putonghua. 'For you.'

'Thank you, Shushu,' Win-win said, bowing his head. Win-win knew about fish cheeks; that was the best, tenderest portion that I always insisted we serve to Ma.

For a moment nobody spoke. Leo's mother set her bowl back onto the table, her lips pursed. She rested her pair of chopsticks across the top of the bowl, apparently finished with her meal, even though we had only just started eating.

'Right,' Melissa said, flustered. She cleared her throat. 'So, Leo, tell us more. How did you two, I mean you three, meet?'

It felt like all eyes were on me and Win-win. I swallowed the piece of sweet and sour pork in my mouth with some difficulty. I downed my cup of tea and suddenly felt a great urge to start coughing.

'I was traveling in Xiamen at the time,' Leo said, once more refilling my teacup as he spoke. 'Pearl showed me around the city, took me to see the best sights.' He shrugged. 'We just hit it off, you know? And Win-win's such a superstar, it was love at first sight.' He held up his hand for a high five, and Win-win gave it to him, but without too much enthusiasm. Even he could sense that we were being judged.

As for me, I was comforted by the way Leo had answered his sister-in-law's question while leaving out all the important parts, the details that were only for us. Remembering the good times — the ferry pier, the *tulou*, the Spiderman scooter, even being at home, shelling peanuts together — it all helped. I reached for my pendant again. *You jump, I jump.* I repeated to myself. *I can do this. I think I can do this.*

His family seemed to be at a loss for words. Leo's dad finally broke the silence: 'Well, I'm really happy–'

'I'm full,' Corrie interrupted, dropping her chopsticks on the table and sliding off her chair. She had only just picked at the food on her plate. At the kindergarten where I worked this would have been grounds for a stern scolding, and she would have been forced to return to the table and finish her meal. 'Yeh Yeh, can I go play video games?'

I was not surprised when Leo's father nodded, what he was about to say forgotten. 'Help me, Daddy,' she ordered.

Henry immediately put down his bowl. He went over to the television and started fiddling with the controls on the game console. Corrie perched on the edge of the sofa, calling out commands. Leo put some more fish in my bowl and kissed me on the temple. 'I'm sorry,' he murmured, in the Min dialect, so only I would understand.

'Mama,' Win-win whispered beside me. 'I'm full, too.' He held up his empty plate to show me. He looked longingly at the television; it was a racing game.

'You go play, too, Win,' Leo said, giving him a little nudge toward Corrie and the TV. 'There are two controllers. You'll show him how, right, Corrie?'

Corrie sighed dramatically. 'Uncle Leo...do I have to?'

'Corrie,' Henry said, sternly. It was the first time I'd heard him speak to his daughter. 'That's no way to behave.'

She rolled her eyes. 'Okay, *fine*. Here, hold this.' She thrust the black controller at Win-win and kept the red for herself. 'Not like *that*,' Corrie said crossly. 'You're messing it up! Press X, not A!'

'Patiently, Corrie,' Melissa calls from the dining table. 'Don't speak so fast. He doesn't understand Cantonese.'

Leo frowned. 'Actually, both Pearl and Win–'

'How is Lindsay doing these days, Melissa?' Pearl's mother

interrupted. 'You must tell her how much we miss having her over.'

Beside me, Leo cleared his throat, as though he was preparing to say something, but Melissa beat him to it. 'I suppose she's alright,' she said, her sighs greatly exaggerated. She and her daughter were so alike. 'She's always telling me how much she misses —' She glanced meaningfully at Leo, who appeared very focused on the shrimp he was peeling. 'Well, all of you. She's been trying to call you, Leo, but...anyhow. She'll be pleased to hear that you still think of her, Nai Nai.'

'How could we not think of her?' Leo's mother cried. 'She was very nearly our daughter-in–'

'Darling,' Leo's father interrupted quietly. He continued in English, but it was clear that he was asking her to stop. I kept my eyes fixed on the peeled shrimp Leo put in my bowl. I stared at it so hard and for so long that it stopped looking like food and just became a striped orange C. Miss Alicia's sing-songy voice came to mind: *C can sound like K. C can sound like S. Add an H, and C can sound like a choo-choo train.* I felt a great urge to laugh. Or maybe cry.

'Well, what? She *was* very nearly our daughter-in-law! And she still wants to be, did you hear that, Leo, she's been trying to call you —'

'*I'm* choosing the level!' Corrie screeched behind us. 'Not you! Stop pressing X! I said *stop!*'

'Indoor voice, please, dear,' Melissa called. 'Isn't she sweet, trying so hard to communicate with your little boy, Pearl —'

I nodded, forcing a smile. 'She's very well-behaved.'

Out of the corner of my eye I could see that Win-win had chosen a turtle-shaped vehicle, and a little monkey for the driver. He hadn't quite got the hang of the game yet; he kept driving his turtle car into the wall.

I turned my attention back to the grown-ups; Leo had switched to English. It was obvious to me that he was trying hard to speak quietly, reasonably, but his mother kept interrupting him, gesticulating wildly with her arms.

She abruptly stood up, her eyes red. 'You'll have to excuse me,' she said, in English, but *excuse me* was one phrase I could understand. 'I'm not feeling well.'

'Nai Nai,' Melissa said, rushing to her. 'Let me walk you to your room.' We watched in silence as the two of them proceeded, arm in arm, to the end of the corridor. The door closed silently behind them.

'Huh,' Henry said, letting out a shaky laugh, 'and then there were four.'

Leo's father sighed. 'I'm sorry, Pearl,' he said, frowning. 'My wife's usually a more gracious host than this.' He hesitated. 'She's been feeling a bit under the weather lately, but there's no excuse for her rudeness. I apologize.'

Just as I was about to respond, a high-pitched wail came from behind us. I spun around, terrified that something terrible had happened to Win-win. But it was Corrie. The four adults still at the table rushed over to the children. Win-win sat on the edge of the sofa, his eyes downcast.

'He pushed me,' she sobbed, clutching her elbow. 'It really *hurts!*'

Henry crouched beside his daughter. 'Corrie, let me see—'

But before he could finish, she had run to the closed bedroom door at the end of the corridor and started banging on it with her fists. 'Mommy! Mommy!' Leo and Henry hurried after her, Henry a few steps behind, an ice pack from the freezer in hand.

The door swung open immediately. 'Oh, sweetheart,' Melissa cried, her voice as high-pitched and hysterical as her daughter's. 'What happened? Are you okay?'

We could hear all this even though we were still in the living room. 'Win-win,' I whispered, wrapping an arm around his shoulders. 'What happened? Did you really push her?'

When Win-win nodded, miserable, my heart sank. I couldn't understand it—it was so unlike Win-win to get physical. 'Why, Win?'

There were tears pooling in his eyes. 'Mama, she–'

'Violence is *not* tolerated in our home.' Leo's mother glared at Win-win as she said this in Cantonese, her tone icy. Corrie whimpered beside her, holding the ice pack to her elbow as though it was broken. 'Under *any* circumstances. This is *unacceptable* behavior.' She turned to face Leo. 'You see what this child has done to our Corrie?'

'Mom—' Leo and Henry glanced at each other, as though surprised that they had spoken at the same time.

'Darling –'

But she ignored both her sons and her husband. 'I am up to here,' she held her hand, palm-down, at eye-level, 'with this nonsense. Your friends are not welcome here, Leo.'

'Go put your shoes on, Win-win,' Leo finally said, staring at his mother. 'We're going home.'

Chapter 24
Leo

Win-win was silent on the taxi ride home, and after a few half-hearted attempts at getting him to speak up, both Pearl and I gave up. He slumped against Pearl, not quite asleep.

'I'm sorry my family was so rude,' I said, leaning over Win-win to kiss Pearl on the forehead. 'Mom especially. I've never seen her like that before. I'm sorry I made you go through that.'

'That's alright,' she said, after a moment. Like her son, she was quiet for the remainder of the journey home.

―――∞―――

Later, when Win-win was changing into his pajamas, I noticed a cluster of dark pink half-moon marks on the back of his right arm, near his elbow, the kind of marks that could really only be formed by fingernails. They weren't noticeable before; they were hidden under his T-shirt sleeve. The Spiderman shirt he was wearing today was a bit too big for him; Pearl had bought one size up so he would be able to grow into it.

Pearl saw the marks at the same time as I did. We exchanged a look over Win's head.

'What happened?' Pearl said, stroking his cheek with her thumb. 'Tell Mama.'

In an uncharacteristic show of defiance, Win-win crossed his arms over his chest. 'No. I won't.'

'What did you say?' She hardened both her expression and her tone.

Win-win cowered at once. 'I...I promised, Mama.'

I held out the pajama bottoms so he could step into them. 'Was it Corrie?'

Win-win gasped, then covered his mouth with both hands. 'Leo Shushu, please don't tell her I said anything. I didn't, did I?'

I gestured to the back of his arm. 'She hurt you here? With her fingernails?'

He nodded, miserable. 'She was upset with me, kept pinching me whenever I did something wrong in the game. She made me promise not to tell or she wouldn't let me play.' He looked pleadingly at his mother. 'Mama, please don't be angry.'

He crawled onto her lap and she held him close. 'Then why did Corrie start crying?'

He sat up at once, ashamed.

'I pushed her. But it was because...the last time she pinched me so hard...so hard and I kept asking her to stop, just quiet you know, so the grown-ups wouldn't hear, because I'd promised I wouldn't tell...but she wouldn't stop, and I pushed her away, just a bit, to get her to stop, but then she bumped her elbow on the coffee table and started crying so loud.' His eyes welled up with tears. 'I'm sorry.'

'You didn't do anything wrong,' Pearl said. Her face crumpled. 'I'm sorry I let you get hurt.' She scooped Win-win up in her arms and took him out to the living room.

'I'm going to call them right now and let them know what

Corrie did,' I said, but no one was listening.

Pearl didn't object when I made Win-win a hot chocolate. I made it warm and sweet, and added extra cream and marshmallows, desperate to do something, anything, to help.

Win-win accepted the mug with two hands and took his first sip. 'It's yummy,' he said, bringing the mug over and over to his lips until there was nothing but a layer of pale brown froth at the bottom. 'Thank you, Leo Shushu. I like it.' He brought the mug to the sink.

'Go brush your teeth again, Win,' Pearl said. 'Then it's time for bed.'

Win-win shuffled to the bathroom.

Pearl reached for my hand. 'Leo...I—'

I couldn't help but interrupt. 'I'm so sorry...I knew it wasn't like Win to push or shove—he's the gentlest child I've ever met–'

She shook her head, her eyes downcast. 'I don't blame you. But I've been thinking—'

'What? What are you thinking?' I could hear the sound of Win-win washing his hands at the bathroom sink.

'Give me a moment,' she said. Behind her, Win-win was standing outside the bathroom door. 'Come here, Win-win. Let's get you in bed.'

She tucked him in and sang him a lullaby in their own dialect, one I hadn't heard before. At the end of the song, she tenderly kissed him on the cheek while I switched off the overhead lights. 'Baba, too,' he murmured groggily, his eyes already closed. 'Baba, too, please.'

I gasped.

'He means you,' she said, her eyes wide. 'He called you Baba!'

I kissed Win-win on the forehead, my heart thundering in my chest. 'I love you, sweet boy,' I whispered. He snored softly in response. I tucked his blanket around his shoulders, ensuring both Simba's and Wuwu's heads were poking out. *My stuffies need to breathe, Uncle Leo,* I heard Corrie's voice pipe up in my head. A serious talk with that young lady was in order.

'Win called me Baba,' I murmured on our way back to the living room. Hearing Win say 'Baba' filled my heart with such joy. Imagine me, a father!

Pearl nodded, but her smile was sad. 'He really loves you.' She sat down on the edge of the sofa, her hands folded. 'Leo, this has been a magical summer. Nothing but magic. And I have loved every moment with you. You have been too good to me. To us.'

Lindsay said very similar things to me when she broke up with me: *These five years have been the best years of my life...it's not you, it's me.* 'You're the one who's been too good to me,' I said, striving to keep my tone light. 'Babe...I know tonight was a disaster. I'm so sorry. We should've left sooner.' I shook my head, trying again. 'We shouldn't have gone at all.'

'I don't blame you,' she repeated softly. 'But we're not teenagers. We can't ignore the way your family feels about me.' She hesitated. 'I know how much you love me and Win-win. I know you would do anything for us...you've already done so much for us—'

'He called me Baba.' I said this quietly, but stubbornly. Didn't that count for anything?

'He did. He really loves you.' She looked away. 'And that's why...we have to do what's best for him, right? I'm not so sure Hong Kong is the best place for him.' She didn't say *You didn't protect Win-win tonight. You let Corrie bully him, and your mother and sister-in-law bully me,* but I could hear it between the lines. She shook her head. 'I'm afraid Hong Kong people's views of mainlanders might be...challenging for Win. For me.'

'Most people here aren't like my mother,' I said quietly. 'Most people aren't like my sister-in-law. A lot of the old prejudices... most people know they aren't true. Pearl, I'm so sorry about tonight. I promise I'll do better. I promise I won't let anybody hurt you ever again, and –'

'How can you promise that?' she asked, her eyes suddenly bright. 'I didn't tell you. But today at the Flower Market someone said 'Go back to where you came from, mainlander' because I was holding up the line.' Her voice trembled then, and it was obvious she was struggling to hold her tears at bay. 'I just stood there and took it. I didn't dare say anything, because I was afraid of what they might do. I don't want Win-win to grow up with that kind of fear. If even your family can't accept us, how can I expect the rest of the city to?'

'Pearl, please, I –'

'I don't blame you.' She repeated this for what I realized was the third time. She cupped my cheek in her hand. 'I love you so much. But I think we need to think some more about where this relationship is going.'

She's breaking up with me. This is the end.

'We were going to go home tomorrow anyhow,' Pearl continued, staring hard at the floor. 'Honestly, since meeting you I haven't been able to think straight. It's like I've been living a fairy tale. But I need to be responsible for my child.'

The child who just called me Baba. I swallowed. 'I—'

'This summer...it's been amazing,' she said, very softly. 'I never imagined it'd be a summer like that.'

I felt cowardly standing there, but there was such finality in her words, I was afraid to say anything that might upset Pearl further. The silence that hung between us felt thick and impenetrable.

'May I shower first?' she finally asked.

Too stunned to speak, I nodded.

A SUMMER LIKE THAT

She was very quick. She emerged from the bathroom with a towel wrapped around her head. She nodded at me, like I was a stranger, then slipped into the bedroom, closing the door behind her.

When I woke up, it was still dark. I found myself spread out on the futon, my limbs sore. It took me a moment to recall the events from the night before, but suddenly it all came back to me at once. The fiasco at Mom and Dad's. The angry red welts on Win-win's arm. The way Pearl said thank you and goodbye.

With a start, I realized the energy in the apartment had shifted. Something wasn't right. I rushed to the bedroom and knocked urgently on the door. When no one answered, I opened the door — just a crack at first, in case they were still asleep — to see that my bed was neatly made, empty. Their carry-on suitcase, which had been parked in the corner of my bedroom since they arrived, was nowhere to be seen.

'Pearl,' I cried. 'Win-win!' No one answered. I glanced at the clock: it wasn't even six o'clock yet. They had already left.

A wave of nausea hit me with such intensity that I barely made it in time to the bathroom. Falling to my knees, I vomited violently into the toilet bowl. As I washed my face, I saw that Pearl had thrown away their toothbrushes; their washcloths had disappeared, too.

I stumbled back into the living room and collapsed onto the sofa, the sofa where Pearl and I had made love for the first time.

This is how it always ends, a voice in my head said sagely. *Did you really think it was going to work out?*

Chapter 25
Pearl

We shouldn't have slunk off the way we did, not after Leo had been so good to us, but that's what we did.

I woke Win-win up at five in the morning, when the sky was still completely dark and when I was certain Leo would still be asleep. I knew he hadn't slept well the night before, because I hadn't either. I pretended to be asleep as I listened to the sounds of him pacing and opening and closing the fridge door. I couldn't bear to talk about us anymore, not when I had already made up my mind.

Win-win protested, then stopped, when I told him Ma wanted us to hurry home; there was an emergency. 'Is she hurt?' he had asked, and in that moment he had looked startlingly grown up.

'It's not that kind of emergency,' I said. 'She's fine. But she needs us to go home right away.'

I felt guilty deceiving him, but I didn't know how to tell him the truth. I was afraid I would lose my resolve if we had to say goodbye to Leo in person. If I heard Win-win call Leo 'Baba' one more time my heart would break.

As we made our way through West Kowloon Station towards

customs, I reminded myself that I was making this decision for Win-win's sake. I glanced at my watch. We would be home before noon. The thought of seeing Ma again propelled me forward.

It wasn't quite six-thirty in the morning, but the station was already quite crowded. The place seemed a lot more intimidating without Leo, but I held Win-win's hand tightly in mine and tried to be brave. *I can do anything*, I thought to myself. *For my son, I can do anything.*

'I need to pee, Mama,' Win-win said, rubbing his eyes with both hands. 'I really need to pee.'

We followed the signs and found the washrooms on our level without any difficulty, but the line was so long—at least ten people ahead of us. I scooped Win-win up and made a dash for the escalators. *Surely there will be fewer people the next floor up*, I thought. *Surely.* I sent up a prayer to Leo's parents' god, since the gods of our village didn't usually take requests without offerings: *Please let us find a toilet! Please let us find a toilet!*

There was no line snaking out of the washrooms on Level 2 the way there was on Level 1. *Thank you*, I began praying, or thinking, as I kept running as fast as I could with one arm holding Win-win against my hip, the way I used to when he was younger, and the other one dragging the carry-on suitcase along behind me.

When we were about ten meters from the washrooms I saw that there was a laminated sign on the door with a message in both Chinese and English: *Closed for cleaning (6-7AM). The nearest washrooms can be found one floor below. We apologize for any inconvenience caused.* I stood there, panting. I stared at the sign, unable to believe what I was reading.

'I really need to go, Mama,' Win pled, holding his knees together. His eyes filled up with tears. 'I can't hold it anymore, I—'

JANE LO

'No, Win! Wait! I have an empty water bottle, wait–'

But he couldn't wait. As he wet his khaki shorts and a puddle formed beneath his feet, he cried and cried. He hadn't had an accident in at least a year and a half. Win-win had always been a quiet crier; his tears fell steadily and his expression was the very definition of misery, but he was silent. 'It's okay, baby, it's not your fault –' I yanked out Win's windbreaker from my backpack and tied it around his waist to hide the dark patch.

Still, we drew attention as I crouched on the floor, mopping up the urine on the floor as best I could with tissues from my backpack. I ended up using the whole pack, but it still wasn't enough. I didn't want to leave a mess behind. Win-win stood beside me, mute.

I kept my voice low, and I spoke in our own dialect – my words were for Win-win's ears only, not the gathering crowd. 'I'll bring you back to Level 1 and you can change into your blue shorts, okay?' They hadn't been washed yet, but this was an emergency. 'Everybody has accidents sometimes. It's okay, darling. It's okay.'

I was stuffing the soiled tissues into a plastic bag when I heard someone's voice from behind me: 'Bet you a hundred bucks those are mainlanders.'

'Yeah,' a second voice agreed. 'We should post photos of them online so they learn to stop treating our city like a public toilet.'

'No, a video!'

I felt angrier than I had ever felt in my life.

'Don't you dare,' I roared, shielding Win-Win from them with my body. 'You leave us alone! *Leave my son alone!*'

'Mainlanders,' they kept muttering, sneering, but to my relief, they wandered off. A janitor finally came with a mop and a bucket.

I squeezed sanitizer onto my hands after I had dropped off

A SUMMER LIKE THAT

the knotted plastic bag in a garbage bin.

'I'm sorry, Mama,' Win-win whispered beside me.

'No need to be sorry,' I said, still seething. 'Accidents happen. You've been such a good boy in Hong Kong, same as always.' He slipped his hand in mine. 'Let's go home.'

After I helped Win-win change out of his soiled shorts, we stopped at Mannings to buy formula for Xiaobei. Ma had asked me to buy as many cans as possible, but I didn't want to risk drawing any more attention to us. I got one can from the shelf and was relieved to find that I had enough Hong Kong dollars left to pay for it. When the cashier asked if I needed a bag, I smiled and shook my head. My accent would give me away as a mainlander for sure.

Finally, it was time to board the train. The steady rhythm of the train was comforting; Win-win yawned as he hugged Wuwu to his chest. His giant Simba, such an expensive and impulsive purchase, was stuffed into my backpack along with Xiaobei's formula. I stroked Win's furrowed brow with my thumb. 'Hey,' I murmured. 'No frowning. We're going home now.'

'But I miss Baba,' he said, his face crumpling. 'I wish we didn't have to go yet.'

I wanted to say *He isn't your Baba*, but didn't want to upset him any further. 'It was time, baby.' I tried to smile. 'We had a good time, didn't we? Sleep now, Win.'

'I miss Baba,' he repeated stubbornly, but he had woken so early that he nodded off before long.

When I was sure that he was asleep, I called Ma. 'We'll be arriving in Xiamen around eleven, Ma. See you soon.'

'Didn't you say tomorrow?' she asked, surprised. 'I told Yong to come get you at the station tomorrow at eleven—isn't that what you said?'

'Yes, but we...ended up getting tickets for today.' I would

explain when I saw her, although I hadn't worked out what exactly I was going to say. Ma would be angry that I had left the way I did. I could predict her exact words: *What does it matter if people are rude? Who cares? It's not just your future on the line. You think you can meet a man like Leo any time you like? And why are you talking like being provided for is a bad thing? It is the best possible thing for a single mother like you...*

Ma hung up after promising to prepare lunch for us. I kept nodding off through the rest of the journey, but couldn't seem to sleep for more than a few minutes. Whenever my thoughts circled back to Leo, I kept myself grounded by glancing at Win-win's sleeping form. I wouldn't have anyone hurting him again.

Since Yong was not at Xiamen Station to pick us up, and there was a tremendously long line at the bus stop—I decided to splurge on a taxi. The ride home filled me with conflicting emotions: the city felt different somehow, more overwhelming and chaotic than I remembered, even though I felt safer here knowing that Win and I belonged.

As the taxi pulled onto our road, I saw Ma standing on the sidewalk, one hand shielding her eyes from the sun, her neck craned. I rolled the window down and Win-win cried, 'Ah Meh! Ah Meh!' over the din of noontime Xiamen traffic. Ma finally spotted our taxi among the many vehicles and began waving at us with gusto.

Ma was as pleased as we hoped she'd be with the Minnie Mouse hat, and kept it firmly on her head, even inside the house. As I wandered from room to room, I found myself feeling discontented with this familiar reality, yet relieved that I had returned to it. Home, which I had always thought was just right for Ma, Win, and me, felt cramped and incomplete. I had forgotten how dim it was inside, how we usually kept the lights switched off during the day. I kept bumping into things.

A SUMMER LIKE THAT

I left Win-win in the kitchen with Ma. She couldn't stop hugging him and kissing him. 'It's been too many days!' she cried. 'Too many!'

I took our bags to my bedroom to unpack, but the first thing I noticed was a pair of rolled-up socks that Leo had left behind on my bedspread. I was surprised to find myself crying as I picked them up and held them in my hands. I heard the chime of a message arriving on my phone and I reached for it — but then I stopped. What if it was Leo? What if it wasn't?

The sound of laughter wafted in from the courtyard. When I looked out the little square window I had looked out of all my life, I saw Win on his scooter with two of the neighbor's children. How good it was to see him among friends again; he must have felt so lonely in Hong Kong, despite all the special outings and meals. Surely it was right for me to come back. I had made the right decision for my son, hadn't I? So why did it feel so wrong?

Ma prepared for us a hearty lunch of meatballs and *mian gua*, a meal I used to adore, but I didn't seem to have much of an appetite. I tried to eat a little, unwilling to give Ma extra reasons to be suspicious. Her probing questions were well-intentioned but hard to bear: *is everything okay? Will you go back to Hong Kong? Didn't you like it there? What happened? Have you broken up?*

I didn't know the answers to these questions. The one question I couldn't stop asking myself was: Had I made the biggest mistake of life?

I finally worked up the courage to check my phone. It was Leo, after all: *Are you okay? Have you gone home? Miss you.* But I didn't know what to say to that. I contemplated responding with a neutral emoji, a thumbs-up maybe, but would that be even worse than not responding? I had never sent him a thumbs-up emoji, ever. I stuffed my phone back into my pocket and decided to worry about it later.

Win-win, usually so easy to please, kept asking for things he couldn't have anymore: a pet rabbit, a visit to the playground by Leo's apartment, those slippery transparent noodles we had with roast goose, Leo himself.

'In Hong Kong,' Win-win said between bites, 'we had noodles with roast goose, not meatballs. You could dip the roast goose in this super yummy orange sauce if you wanted. I ate the sauce with a spoon like it was taro mud!'

Ma laughed, unbothered by this apparent comparison to her cooking. 'You liked Hong Kong a lot, didn't you, Win?'

'Sure,' he agreed. 'Baba... I mean—' here he glanced at me, 'Leo Shushu...he took us to Disneyland, Ah Meh! That's where we got your hat! And he took us to see the hamsters and the bunny rabbits and the lady at the store even let me feed the bunny some pellets with a wooden spoon—'

Later that afternoon, after Win-win had gone next door to play, I sat down to trim peas with Ma. I was afraid she would try to ask more questions, since I hadn't managed to answer any to her satisfaction, but I needn't have worried; she had the television on and was watching *Meet Your Match*. I couldn't believe how much I used to like this programme, to *believe* it. Today, I just wanted to switch it off, but Ma seemed as engrossed as ever, and I supposed enduring the programme was better than trying to explain why things had ended so abruptly with Leo, especially when Win-win couldn't stop raving about him. My pile of trimmed peas was considerably smaller than Ma's, even though her eyes were fixed on the television screen. I was pretty quick with my hands, I'd been doing these chores since I was a little girl, but I was no match for Ma. She could trim peas in her sleep.

We had watched this episode a hundred times. 28-year-old Meiyun, a petite nurse from Qingdao, was about to say yes to a kind-faced, heavy-set acupuncturist, 34, from Changsha. As they linked arms, the crowd went wild. Ma picked up the remote control and turned the volume all the way down so that all the clapping and cheering died down immediately. She reached for another pea and expertly removed, in one swift movement, both the tag and the string. 'That could have been you,' she muttered. 'This was supposed to be your happy ending, finally.'

I kissed her gently on the cheek. 'Ma, I'm sorry it didn't work out. Really, I'm sorry.'

And I meant it—my heart was aching and all I wanted to do was lie down and forget that this summer had ever happened. Cinderella experiences were too much for people like me. I had no business imagining a fairytale ending; it was way out of my league. And to have involved Win-win in it all...I would never forgive myself for being so irresponsible. *Baba!* What had I been thinking, bringing Win-win to Hong Kong like that? What kind of mother was I?

No matter, I thought resolutely to myself. School would be starting in a few weeks, and both Win and I would be back at the kindergarten. Ma would get to work planting peanuts, sweet potatoes, mustard greens. Life would continue. I reached up to stroke my cactus pendant with my thumb, then went for the clasp instead. I took it off and held it in a tight fist, wondering why I hadn't left it in Hong Kong where it belonged.

Sighing heavily, Ma switched off the television.

Chapter 26
LEO

When I opened my eyes again, it was past noon. There was a dull ache reverberating at the base of my neck, and the back of my head, like someone had hit me, hard. I winced as I sat up. I thought of the way Pearl placed her hands on my head and removed my headache that morning, like magic. If she were here beside me I wouldn't let her do anything for me, I would just hold her and love her and beg her for another chance. With a start I realized my phone was ringing. My heart leapt with hope — it had to be Pearl.

The voice in my head piped up right away. *Why would she call you now, when she has taken such pains to leave without speaking to you?* I didn't want to entertain that question and focused on getting up from the floor and reaching the bedroom, where the ringtone continued, insistent.

The number was hidden. It *had to* be Pearl — numbers from the mainland didn't always show up, and perhaps her phone was out of batteries and she was using a relative's phone.

'Pearl?' I said. 'Did you make it home okay? You and Win left in such a hurry —'

On the other end of the line was someone breathing, but there was something distinctive — something *off* about the breathing — and with a chill I realized that it wasn't Pearl at all. 'Where are you? Is someone there with you?'

More labored breathing. It sounded worse than it had even a moment ago. 'Leo — '

The line went dead.

I grabbed my keys from the coffee table and rushed out the door.

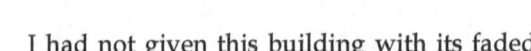

I had not given this building with its faded blue paint, this dim elevator, a single moment's thought in weeks, but my fingers knew which buttons to press on the security code panel: 8729. My heart, which had up to this point been fully consumed by Pearl, knew to hammer in my chest out of worry for Lindsay. It knew this was an emergency.

The elevator ride took much longer than I felt it should — but when the elevator doors snapped apart on the 12th floor; my feet immediately remembered to turn left; Lindsay lived in Flat H. I used to think *husband* every time I saw the H outside her flat. Remembering that made me feel stupid all over again.

I was brought back to the present when I saw her front door was ajar. 'Lindsay?' I called. There was no answer. 'Lindsay!'

'I'm coming in!' I pushed the door open. Even though it was early in the afternoon, the apartment was dark: the curtains were drawn, the lights switched off. I patted the wall for the light switches, finally locating them. Immediately I saw where she was: in the kitchen, slumped against the refrigerator on the tile floor. I rushed over to her. She was taking frantic, shallow breaths, her chest rising and falling erratically.

'Hey,' I said, crouching beside her. 'You don't look so good.

Where's your inhaler?' I gave the kitchen a quick scan for her purse; she always used to keep her Ventolin in the front pocket.

'You — came,' she gasped. She grabbed at my arms; her hands were clammy, ice-cold. When she rested her head on my shoulder, the wheezing in her chest was so loud it was like a whistle. 'I — knew you would — come for me, Leo, I-'

'Lindsay,' I said, more firmly. 'Where's your inhaler?'

She looked at me with an expression I couldn't read. 'Left it — at -w-work.'

I punched 999 into my phone.

The paramedics arrived at Lindsay's door with a collapsible wheelchair in less than ten minutes. One opened it up while the other lifted Lindsay off the floor; she was so light that it seemed to take no effort at all. She didn't used to be quite so thin. Her lips were now tinged with blue.

I climbed in the front of the ambulance with the driver as the paramedics tended to Lindsay in the back. 'Your wife?' The driver asked, glancing at me in the rearview mirror.

'Family friend.'

This seemed to be a reasonable enough response; the driver nodded, turning his focus back on the road.

I called my brother, who picked up on the second ring. 'Leo?'

The ambulance sped past a yellow light. 'Lindsay's having an asthma attack; we're on an ambulance. Is Melissa with you?'

'That's terrible,' he said. 'Hold on. I'll go get her.'

A moment later, Melissa came onto the line. 'What's going on? Is Lindsay okay?'

'I think so.' Behind me I could hear the muffled sounds of the paramedics speaking in soothing tones to Lindsay. 'The ambulance came right away. We're nearly at Princess Margaret.

Can you please come?' I was suddenly terrified that she might not be available and I would have to stay with Lindsay on my own. 'I...I can't stay too long.'

'Of course. I'll ask Henry to call me an Uber.'

At the hospital Lindsay and her oxygen tank bypassed the queue; her wheelchair was pushed directly into the ER, although the waiting area was more than half-full of people waiting for medical attention. A grey quilt had been tucked around her, and she looked more like an invalid than ever.

'You wait here,' one of the paramedics cried, clapping me on the shoulder. 'Hey, chin up, man. She's going to be fine.' They waved goodbye before climbing back into the ambulance.

A few minutes later, Melissa arrived, a bulging tote bag slung over her shoulder. She plopped down on the plastic chair beside mine. 'I can't believe this is even happening. She hasn't had an attack in years.' She patted the tote bag. 'I brought some stuff she might need if she has to stay the night. You know...slippers, headphones, stuff like that.'

I'd never been so happy to see my sister-in-law. 'Thanks. We left in such a hurry she hasn't got anything with her, just her wallet and her phone.'

She looked at me curiously. 'What were you doing in her flat?'

'She called me,' I said, trying not to sound defensive. 'She couldn't breathe. Didn't have her inhaler with her.'

Melissa stared at me, and I had the strange sense that I had been duped somehow. But Lindsay couldn't have faked her asthma attack; I saw her condition with my own eyes. Her lips were blue. She could have died. No one could fake that.

'She's really sorry, you know,' she said, after a moment. 'That mess with her coworker was...a mistake. She can't stop talking about how sorry she is.'

When I didn't answer, she continued: 'Where are your... friends?'

I didn't want to answer this, not with Pearl so far away, in more ways than one. 'Pearl and Win-win—' I swallowed hard. I looked away; my eyes were smarting and the last thing I wanted to do was to cry in front of Melissa. 'They...they had to go back to Xiamen.'

'You don't look too pleased about that,' she said. 'You really like her, huh? But are you sure she wasn't a rebound–'

Just then an orderly in faded blue scrubs pushed Lindsay back out into the waiting area. We quickly grabbed our bags and joined her. 'Hey guys,' she said, beaming. It was a relief to see that she was no longer gasping for breath, although her complexion was still very pale. 'Fancy seeing you here!'

'This isn't funny! You scared me to death, you crazy woman,' Melissa cried, fretting over Lindsay like she was a little girl. I saw the way they exchanged a look before glancing at me. I pretended not to notice. I felt my phone buzz in my pocket and was about to reach for it when Lindsay placed her hand on my forearm.

'Thank you for coming to help me, Leo,' she said, shyly. She made a movement like she was tucking hair behind her ear, but her hair was too short to tuck. Lindsay was a poor imitation of Pearl.

'That's alright.' I cleared my throat. 'I'm glad you're feeling better now.'

'Leo, I—' She slid her hand down the length of my arm and tried to weave her fingers through mine, the way we always used to hold hands—and for a moment I almost let her, not because I loved her anymore, but because she was just in the ER. But at the last moment I stuffed my hands back into my pockets. 'I just want to say–'

A SUMMER LIKE THAT

The orderly, who had been watching us with some interest, rescued me: 'Actually, ma'am, I need to take you up to the ward now.'

'I just need one moment with my…friend,' Lindsay said, and even now, pale as she was, she was able to flash the orderly such a persuasive, pleading smile that he couldn't help but smile back at her. She coughed weakly. 'It's…he's…very important.'

'Well, alright.' He scratched the back of his neck. 'But not too long. The nurses upstairs will be wondering where I took you.'

Melissa squeezed Lindsay's shoulder. 'I need to call Hen real quick, make sure he remembers to bring Maa Maa's gift to the party tonight. I'll stay with you till it's time for dinner, okay?'

Lindsay nodded, smiling up at me, pleased to have gotten her way. She'd always had that power over people, but the line between being charming and manipulative was a fine one. I missed Pearl's refreshing authenticity — although sometimes it hurt. 'Will you push me over there?' She gestured towards the far end of the waiting area, which was now empty.

Locking the brakes on her wheelchair, I sat down beside her. 'What did you want to tell me?'

'Leo, it isn't really over between us, is it?' As if on cue, her eyes filled with tears.

'Hey,' I said, looking down at my hands. There was a hangnail on my left index finger that was getting a bit inflamed. I resisted the urge to rip it off. 'Don't do this.'

'You still love me,' she insisted, her cheeks tear-stained and splotchy. 'You were so worried about me. You dropped everything to come help me. You wouldn't do that for just anyone.' She crossed her arms over her chest. 'What happened this summer — I don't care. I don't mind that you had a summer fling with that mainland woman. I…I forgive you.'

I looked at this woman that I had loved so deeply, for so long.

Had she always been like this?

'I came because you couldn't breathe.' I said. 'It wasn't because I still have feelings for you. Look, the orderly's waiting. Melissa, too.'

Her face crumpled and she began crying openly. I sensed people's eyes on me as I pushed Lindsay's wheelchair through the waiting area back to the entrance of the ER.

I was very relieved to pass Lindsay back to the orderly. Melissa rubbed Lindsay's back, murmuring, 'Never mind, never mind,' under her breath.

'See you,' I said, but no one responded.

On my MTR ride back home, I got a call from a number I didn't recognize and I nearly declined it, but when I picked up, I was surprised to find that it was Miss Penny from the kindergarten we visited the day before. 'Hi, is that Mr. Leung? This is Miss Penny from Sham Tseng Nursery School.'

I would recognize her bright sing-songy voice anywhere. 'Yes, hello.' I could hear the tinkling music of the kindergarten in the background.

'I hope this isn't too forward of me,' she began, 'but I just wanted to tell you how much I enjoyed meeting the little boy you brought to visit our school yesterday morning.'

'Thank—thank you,' I stammered, wondering where this conversation was going.

'I wondered if you might be able to pass on this message to Win-win's mother—he made quite the impression on me and the other teachers... and I'm not sure what his family's plans are for the coming academic year, but I just wanted him to know that he would be very, very welcome to join us in K2 in September.'

I was taken aback by this news, but delighted too. Might Pearl reconsider if she knew how well Win-win had done even in a casual school tour? Would she give him—no, them—a chance?

'I'll definitely let his mom know. He won't need to attend an interview?' This was unheard of.

She let out a conspiratorial little laugh. 'I'm afraid I already asked him quite a lot of questions and observed him as he was trying out the different toys and equipment on the roof. He was exceptionally well-mannered and inquisitive, and would be such a welcome addition to our school.'

This was so good to hear, but I had one nagging doubt. 'Even without Cantonese? Without English?'

'Yes. I have no worries about that. It's obvious he'll adapt quickly.'

I couldn't wait to tell Pearl and Win-win, but when I tried to video-call them, it asked me to leave a message. I wanted to tell them directly rather than in a recorded message, so I declined. I would try again later.

I glanced at my watch. Aunt Tammy may have written 7 p.m. on the mass Whatsapp invitation she had sent everyone, but I knew better. Nobody would be showing up later than 6:30 to Grandma's birthday party, and even that would be considered borderline late. I planned on arriving extra early, of course; Grandma would want me to help pass out red packets to everyone, and help welcome relatives as they arrived. Perhaps Melissa would be late this year, since she had been at the hospital all day with Lindsay.

I shrugged on my red and white shirt, the only red article of clothing I owned. My extended family was big on auspicious colors; last year my cousin Matt wore a navy dress shirt to Grandma's birthday dinner and the aunts made him change out of it. One of them had brought a few spare red polo shirts to avert any potential disasters. 'I knew we'd use at least one,' Aunt

Tammy had said, smugly.

Pearl sent me one message: *Thank you for the trip to Hong Kong, goodbye* but had ignored all of my replies, from *How was your journey home?* to *Is it okay to call?*

I slipped two $500 bills into the special red envelope I picked out for Grandma at the stationery store, the one with two golden peaches. Above the peaches were eight characters, the quintessential birthday blessings: *May your fortunes be boundless, like the Eastern Sea, and your longevity as enduring as the Southern Mountains.* I added my own birthday message to the back of the envelope with a Sharpie.

I half-ran, half-walked from Shek Mun MTR station and arrived at Club One Riviera at 6:17. The sun was just beginning to set. After a moment's hesitation, I stopped to take a picture of the restaurant for Pearl. It was a good shot—it looked like we were dining on an actual boat, when in reality, the 'floating restaurant' was just a pretty building designed to resemble a small cruise ship floating on Shing Mun River. I didn't wait for her response—it might not come at all—and stepped into the building.

The elevator jolted to a stop and the doors slid open. A server greeted me at the entrance with a nod and a slight bow before leading me to the biggest private room at the end of the restaurant, the one with *Leung Family Birthday Banquet* flashing in rainbow on the LED screen outside. The server nodded once more before leaving me to enter the room on my own. For a moment I wondered what it would have been like to have Pearl beside me, Win-win clutching my hand. My eyes smarted at the thought of them. Was it really over for us?

'I'm over here, Piglet!' Grandma crowed from her wheelchair. I used to hate this childhood nickname—I was rather pudgy as a child, and it took a great many hours at the gym to get to my

A SUMMER LIKE THAT

current state — but I didn't mind it anymore.

The party was well underway: three mahjong tables had been set up along one side of the room, both my parents at one of them with two of my aunts. Everyone was noisily shuffling tiles, raucous laughter breaking out every few moments. I had always been a bit shocked by how at ease everyone was once they were around a mahjong table. The little ones, Corrie included, were belting out *Let It Go* on the karaoke system as their doting mothers looked on. Corrie was wearing a frilly pink Aurora dress today, and appeared to be bossing the other kids around, as usual. When Corrie saw me, she started waving — then abruptly stopped when she saw my glacial expression. I would be having a talk with that young lady before the night was through. The dads stood behind their wives, no doubt discussing the stock market.

Henry, who was chatting with my cousin Matt, gave me a little wave. I was about to wave back when Grandma impatiently repeated, 'Over *here*, Piglet!'.

Her wheelchair was in the corner of the room, where she had a clear view of everything, and several chairs had been positioned around her so her children and grandchildren could present their gifts and chat with her before dinner was served. She eyed the mahjong tables longingly; she used to play every day with her buddies, but in the last few years her arthritis had gotten progressively worse. Eventually she had struggled too much with the slippery tiles to enjoy the game. Her mind was still crystal clear, though.

She was dressed to the nines tonight in a rose gold cheongsam and matching shawl; her silver hair was permed, the curls held back with a rose gold tiara, no doubt Corrie's idea. Even Grandma's nails were painted rose gold. 'Just yourself tonight?'

I shrugged, having anticipated this question. 'Yup, just me

tonight, Grandma. Happy Birthday,' I responded smoothly, kissing her cheek. My cousin Andy shot me a questioning look; everyone had loved Lindsay, and anyway, *he* had brought his girlfriend, a nervous-looking young woman whose facial features were obscured by various pieces of metal: thick wire-rimmed glasses, a nose ring, braces. Andy vacated the seat beside Grandma so I could sit down.

Someone had hired a professional photographer, a smiling young man dressed entirely in black apart from a shocking pink tie and suspenders. He focused his enormous SLR camera on Grandma and me the moment I sat down. 'Big smiles this way, please! And 3...2...1...*cheese!*'

'Good health and long life, Grandma,' I continued, once the photographer had proclaimed the picture the very best of the night, 'and the very happiest of birthdays.'

She pursed her lips, pretending to pout. 'Not likely, not since you've come on your own.'

I patted her wrinkled hand in what I hoped was a comforting gesture. 'Who else do you want to see? Grandma, *I'm* your favorite, remember?'

'Yes, of course,' she agreed, a twinkle in her eye. 'And that's my point exactly.' Her voice dropped to a conspiratorial whisper: 'You know I didn't give my wedding bangles to Melissa, just bought her and Henry something else. I'm saving my dragon and phoenix bangles for *you*, Piglet. You going to keep this old woman waiting around forever?'

'Grandma,' I suddenly blurted out. 'Lindsay and I broke up at the start of the summer. It wasn't working out.' I wasn't sure why I was saying this to my grandmother on her ninetieth birthday. I swallowed hard. 'But I met someone else.'

If my grandmother was startled by this news, she hid it well. 'Tell me more,' she said, leaning in so she could hear better.

A SUMMER LIKE THAT

'Tell me the rest.'

And so I did. Grandma listened quietly, attentively. Finally, when the words began to run dry, I showed her a picture of Pearl on my phone, the one of her in the white dress, posing in front of the cactuses at the Botanical Garden.

She reached for the reading glasses hanging on a beaded cord around her neck and peered at the screen. 'Pretty,' she pronounced, nodding. 'She's got an honest face.'

'She's so lovely, Grandma,' I said, stuffing my phone back into my pocket. 'I really wish I could have brought her to meet you tonight.'

'Why didn't you?'

'She's gone home. She's from Xiamen.'

She didn't seem to hear the part about her being from the mainland, or maybe she didn't care. 'Not for good, though, right? You can bring her another time. We can go for dimsum. Does she like dimsum?'

'Maybe for good.' I was on the verge of tears. 'I'm not sure, Grandma.'

'If you love her,' she said, 'you have to go after her. Quick, too.' She leaned in even closer, lowered her voice. 'Want to bring the phoenix bangles with you? Bring them with you, see what she thinks.'

When I kissed her on the cheek, I caught a faint whiff of her Olay face cream, the same kind she had used since I was a child. I felt a great surge of affection for my grandmother, who was so very wise and loved me so much. 'You give her the bangles yourself. I want to introduce her to you.' Just before I stood up to make room for the next well-wisher, I held out my red packet to her, with two hands. 'This is for the birthday girl.'

She received it with a smile, patting her hair coyly. 'The best gift you can give this old woman is good news. I'll be waiting for it!'

When I turned around, I felt a tap on my shoulder. 'I'll drive you,' Henry said quietly. 'I overheard what you were saying to Grandma. I'll drive you to West Kowloon Station after the party. You've got your home-return permit in your wallet, haven't you?'

I stared at him, shocked. 'Sure, but–'

'Then we'll go.' He nodded, the matter settled. 'I support you. I'm sorry I didn't stand up for you or Pearl, or her little boy, that night at Mom and Dad's. Mom and Mel can make quite the nasty pair. But I certainly didn't help.'

He could say that again. But I was so grateful, all was forgiven.

Dad sent me a message shortly after midnight, a message that made me tear up: *You have my support, son. Now and always. Tell little Win-win I have more candy waiting for him when he comes back to HK.*

The train pulled into Xiamen a little after 3 a.m. in the morning. I managed to book a room at the same hotel as last time. I took a shower and climbed into bed. The next morning I would need to buy a change of clothes; I hadn't brought anything with me other than my phone and wallet.

Lying here in the silence, I realized, for the first time, that despite how devastated I had felt when Lindsay broke things off with me, I never tried to get back together with her. Why was that?

With the clarity of a person who had just recovered from a crushing migraine, it became clear that some part of me had known all along that Lindsay was not the one. She had never been the one.

My heart felt buoyant and light as my eyes finally drooped

shut.
>	I had a plan.

Chapter 27
Pearl

I stood at my usual spot, just left of the phone booth. It had been a slow day at the ferry pier, only two clients in the morning and one in the afternoon. The work had been surprisingly dull — I used to love introducing the history of Gulangyu to tourists, but none of the tourists had seemed all that interested, and to be honest, my heart wasn't really in it either. It made me think of meeting Leo — and it hurt to think of him. The cloudy, moody weather hadn't helped; the clouds looked swollen with rain and smog. It wasn't even four yet, but I decided to call it a day.

When Ma got out the peanuts and switched on the TV to watch *Meet Your Match* last night, I slunk off to bed, pretending to have a headache. I *did* have a headache; since coming back to Xiamen my body ached along with my heart. But the real reason was that I was still not ready to celebrate other people's happy endings yet. Maybe I was done with *Meet Your Match* for good.

Things with Ma had been frosty since yesterday; she was insistent that I had made a mistake, the biggest mistake of my life. *I just want to understand,* she kept saying. *A well-educated man loves you, wants to marry you. He's promised to provide for you and*

A SUMMER LIKE THAT

Win-win, to give you a future. What more could you want, Pearl?

Not wanting her to worry, I had downplayed the fiasco at Leo's parent's home and the nasty remarks people made about me at the Flower Market and at West Kowloon Station — but I did this so well that she thought I was just overreacting. *Those aren't reasons at all. You're being too sensitive.*

She finally stopped asking her questions when I broke down, crying, and told her how Win-win had wet his pants at the train station, and how people had threatened to film him. *I don't want him to feel small all his life, Ma. And living in Hong Kong, jobless, will make me feel small too. Can't you understand that?*

As I was packing my visor and neck fan into my backpack, I heard a clap of thunder above my head; the sky had turned a menacing slate grey. Fat raindrops begin to fall with growing urgency. I scrambled to pull out my fold-up umbrella.

Abruptly, the rain stopped falling on me. When I looked up, I saw that someone was holding a striped black and white umbrella over me, shielding me from the rain. I blinked at it, confused. How had it gotten up there?

'Excuse me,' a voice said behind me. I should have been startled, but I wasn't. I knew that voice. I...

'Would you happen to know where I can catch a ferry for Gulangyu?'

I gasped. When I turned around, I felt like I'd been transported back in time. It was the beginning of the summer; we were meeting for the first time.

It was Leo — Leo with the patchy, unloved beard and the kind eyes, the battered watch on his wrist. We were standing so close to each other that it was apparent to me that he smelled exactly the way I remembered: soapy and clean and safe. Around us the rain kept falling and falling, a steady, relentless downpour, but under the umbrella, we were dry and unharmed.

'Pearl,' he said, softly.

I stood there, mute, blinking and blinking until I couldn't hold the tears back anymore.

He dug in his backpack and handed me a tissue. Even this part was the same. 'It's peach,' I thought, then realized I had spoken aloud. 'It's still peach.'

'Do you think...you can give me – us – another chance?'

This came out so baldly, so earnestly, that I couldn't speak. I thought of that woman, Lindsay, and how she had broken his heart. How could I do the same to him? And yet...

'I want to,' I whispered, 'but I'm so afraid.'

'I promise I'll do better,' he said anxiously, 'I won't let anyone hurt you or Win-win ever again, and if anybody tries–'

'But your family–'

'Pearl, look.' With a trembling hand, he unlocked his phone. When he held it out to me, I saw on the screen a gleaming pair of bracelets resting in a velvet box. They appeared to be of solid gold, about two inches wide. Each bracelet featured a dragon and a phoenix. The eye of each phoenix was a ruby. I knew what they were, what they represented.

'These are bridal bangles,' I said, softly.

'My Grandma wouldn't let Henry have them,' he said, peering at the picture over my shoulder. 'He wanted them for Melissa, but Grandma said they were for my bride. I know it's early days yet,' he added hastily, 'but Pearl...I just want you to know I'm not messing around. I'm serious. I've never been so serious in my life.'

I opened my mouth to speak, but Leo wasn't finished.

'And my family – they were horrid that night, just beastly, but it won't happen again. Dad, and my brother Henry – they support us. My Grandma, too, and she's the big boss. My mother...Melissa...I promise I'll talk to them. And if they're going to keep being like this, we won't see them again until they can be kind.'

'Leo, I–'

'Wait,' he cried, unwilling to give me another chance to protest. 'Please, let me show you one more thing.'

He opened his backpack a second time and reached deep within. 'I thought about just taking a picture, but I thought you might want to check the size yourself.'

I was afraid that he was about to present me with an engagement ring – but what he held out to me was children's clothing. With a start I realized it was a school uniform – a white polo shirt with a red collar and cuffs, a pair of khaki shorts with an elastic waistband, and little red socks. 'It's early, it's early,' Leo repeated, embarrassed, 'but Miss Penny called, and I was just so excited.'

I felt my heart hammering in my chest. 'You don't mean... Miss Penny from the kindergarten? Why did she call you?'

Leo smiled, but I could see that he was blinking back tears. 'Win-win impressed her so much that even though it wasn't an official interview, she could see that he had the qualities they were looking for in their students. She said they'd absolutely love to welcome him at the school. He's such a good boy, Pearl. The best.'

My clever boy! Maybe Win would survive, no, thrive, in Hong Kong after all, if the principal of a kindergarten thought he would...

'I think he would do very well there,' he added, softly. 'I think he would be happy. Happy and safe. We could get that rabbit he liked so much at Pet Street, and plants, lots and lots of plants...and I did some research on the train ride over – it's not uncommon for new immigrants to find work in Shenzhen. You could be a tour guide if you want, or work at a kindergarten like before—'

'How did you know I want to find a job in Hong Kong?' I hadn't mentioned that to Leo, not directly.

He smiled. 'I know how much you want to provide for Win-win yourself. You don't want to be a burden. But Pearl…you could never be a burden to me.' When he reached out to embrace me, I didn't resist. 'Give me another chance,' he whispered. 'Please, baby. Can you give us another chance?'

This is my happy ending. It's okay. It's okay for me to have my happy ending. I don't have to fight this. I can be independent, but I can also be loved. I can be both.

I cupped Leo's scratchy chin in my hand, and when he closed his eyes, I felt the weight of his love for me in my hand and heart. *I love you*, I thought, and I did, so much, that tears came.

'Yes,' I whispered, pressing my lips against his. 'Yes.'

About The Author

Jane Lo is a Chinese-Canadian writer and English teacher. Shortly after she was born in Hong Kong, her family moved to Vancouver. In university she studied Biblical Hebrew and English Literature and loved both: she pursued further studies in one (Hebrew) and a career teaching the other (English). Over the years she has worked and studied in both cities, but she is now happily settled in Hong Kong with her husband and two children. Her passions include reading detective mysteries and writing happily-ever-afters. *A SUMMER LIKE THAT* is her second novel.

www.ingramcontent.com/pod-product-compliance
Lightning Source LLC
LaVergne TN
LVHW030320070526
838199LV00069B/6514